INDIAN CARPETS

E. Gans-Ruedin

INDIAN CARPETS

Photographs by Leo Hilber
Translated by Valerie Howard

RIZZOLI
NEW YORK

Drawings by RONALD SAUTEBIN

French-language edition, *Le Tapis des Indes*
Copyright © 1984 by Office du Livre S.A., Fribourg, Switzerland

English translation:
Copyright © 1984 by Office du Livre S.A., Fribourg, Switzerland

Published in 1984 in the United States of America by:

*R*IZZOLI INTERNATIONAL PUBLICATIONS, INC.
712 Fifth Avenue/New York 10019

Library of Congress Cataloging in Publication Data

Gans-Ruedin, E. (Erwin)
Indian carpets.

Translation of Le Tapis des Indes.
Bibliography: p.
Includes index.
1. Rugs—India.   I. Title.
NK2876.A1G3613   1984   746.7'54   84-42716
ISBN 0-8478-0551-4

Printed and bound in West Germany

CONTENTS

To the creators of these magnificent carpets – the anonymous Indian weavers

PREFACE

The origins of the hand-knotted carpet can be traced back more than two thousand years. Even today, with the abundance of technical aids and mechanical and electronic looms at our disposal, this ancestral process has not been superseded. It is unique in having preserved its form and style throughout the course of history, while never losing its essential value. Traditional patterns recur on carpets woven throughout the Orient, from Asia Minor to China, and arouse the same admiration whatever their source. Museums the world over have paid large sums to add outstanding hand-knotted carpets to their collections.

In India the hand-knotted carpet appeared in the fifteenth century and, after its introduction into Kashmir, rapidly attained a high degree of perfection. Like the carpets of Iran, Indian carpets reached the height of splendour in the sixteenth and seventeenth centuries under the Mughal emperors, who unified India and whose taste for luxury provided a favourable environment for commerce and the arts.

Later on, political conflicts and military conquests relegated the development of arts and crafts to the background. It was not until the Great Exhibition of 1851 in London that the carpet-making art was revived in India and, from then on, captivated the Western market. English companies set up looms at Srinagar, Amritsar, Mirzapur and elsewhere. But unfortunately, the importers attempted to impose their own patterns and, in order to reduce manufacturing costs, provided poor-quality wool. And so Indian carpets, which in the past had been distinguished by harmony of motifs and brilliance of colouring, became dull and uniform; to satisfy the obsession of the day for the 'antique', they were even subjected to an artificial fading process.

Today, especially since the end of World War II, the situation has undergone a complete transformation. A skilled work-force, trained in government-sponsored schools, produces rugs fit to rival the products from the most highly regarded sources. It is not unusual to find an Indian carpet with a knot-count in excess of 500,000 per square metre (323 per square inch) and made of imported wools of superior quality which produce a lustrous pile.

The artistic past of India is so fruitful that present-day production centres can draw in abundance on motifs that contributed to the beauty of Indian carpets in former days; thus, in Kashmir, the patterns of early Kashmiri shawls are now being reproduced.

Few books speak of the Indian carpet, save for those actually published in that country at the beginning of this century: C. Latimer (1906), N. G. Mukerji (1907), H. T. Harris (1908) and A. and C. Black (published in London in 1900). K. Erdmann, in his *Siebenhundert Jahre Orientteppich* (1966), devotes only a few lines to them, but M.S. Dimand in *Oriental Rugs in the Metropolitan Museum of Art* (1973) dedicates a whole chapter to the Mughal rugs in the seventeenth century. In addition, because of its interesting nature, a small work by Kamaladevi Chattopadhyaya, *Carpets and Floor Coverings of India*, was published by the Ministry of Commerce of the Indian government in 1969.

The aim of this work is to provide readers with information as complete as possible on the production of the hand-knotted carpet in India as it is conceived today by the major centres in the country, while at the same time introducing them to examples from the Mughal period and the nineteenth century.

HISTORICAL SURVEY

India, it seems, was unknown to Europeans until the campaigns of Alexander the Great in the fourth century BC, and present-day research provides us with only scant information on prehistoric India. The civilizations that had taken root in the Indus and the Ganges valleys in the fourth millennium BC competed with those flourishing in Sumer and Egypt—all striving to exercise their ascendancy. Northern India was invaded by the Aryans, a small tribe from central Asia that infiltrated as far as Europe. Brahmanism evolved from the Vedic religion of these invaders.

For the Hindus, the political history of India begins with a great epic account known as the *Mahābhārata* that relates the struggles waged on the banks of the Yamuna between the sons of Kuru, bloodthirsty warriors who had come down from the north, and the sons of Pāndu, the peace-loving inhabitants of the country.

In *The Early History of India* (1908), Vincent A. Smith expresses the opinion that the earliest facts acceptable on an historically sound basis date from the seventh century BC, when maritime trade increased and the art of writing began to spread. First the Persians, then the Greeks invaded India from the north-west. The Persian king Cyrus the Great (d. 529 BC) took Kāpica, and Darius I (d. 486 BC) annexed Gandhāra and the Lower Indus valley (517-16). But their conquests were short-lived. In 326 BC Alexander the Great triumphed over King Pōros. He left behind garrisons and established colonies in the country, but his achievements, although apparently soundly based, did not survive him.

The village of Lumbini near Kapilavastu, capital of the Sākya clan, was privileged to be the birthplace of Siddharta Gautama (*c.* 556-*c.* 480), known as Cākyamuni or Buddha, that is to say 'the Enlightened One'. Buddhism was to attract many disciples. A semi-historical contemporary of the Buddha was Jina ('the Victor'), the founder of Jainism.

One of the rulers of the Maurya dynasty (*c.* 325-*c.* 183 BC), Asoka, who seems to have reigned from 264 to 227 or 226, became converted to Buddhism. He was obsessed with morals; thus all his writings took the form of edicts. According to tradition, he was a contemporary of the Chinese emperor Qin Shihuangdi under whose reign the Great Wall was built. Asoka's influence extended over a considerable area of the Deccan, the peninsula of India south of the Narmada River. In southern India, traces of his sagacious texts have even been found inscribed on pillars or bare rock faces in *Brahmi* script. To this day this good prince, who ruled his states with justice and wisdom and raised Buddhism to a state religion, is venerated throughout India.

During the fourth century AD, the Hindu Gupta Empire (*c.* 320-550) came into being in northern and central India. In the eyes of historians and linguists, the reign of the Guptas brought the civilization of ancient India to its apogee. Schools were created, and the arts and sciences were fostered to such extent that, in this field, the Guptas were in advance of the rest of the world. This was the golden age of India.

The technical arts, astronomy and mathematics flourished equally under the patronage of the Guptas. Sanskrit literature became widespread and contributed in no small measure to the moulding of the Hindu spirit. Art was first and foremost religious. It set out to express the transcendence of the Divine in concrete form. Two artistic trends coexisted with each other: the Brahmanic school, which sculpted, painted and modelled a powerful god of imposing majesty; and the Buddhist school, which portrayed a divinity whose radiant countenance conveyed serenity and mercy.

Moreover, this was the period when Buddhism spread throughout Asia, trailing with it elements of Indian civilization, in particular Indian art, which was at its peak of achievement at that time; purity of form and harmony of proportions were combined in perfect balance. Temples of rare beauty appeared, constructed of durable materials, such as those at Sānchi and the one dedicated to Dūrga at Aihole.

The Chinese Buddhists who came on pilgrimage to India for several centuries considered it to be their 'Holy Land'. The earliest of these known to us is Faxian, who arrived in India in AD 399 and lived there for fifteen years. On his return to China, in *Record of Buddhistic Kingdoms* (which has been translated into English and French), he described the adventures of his journey, providing valuable information on the system of government and the conditions of life in the provinces of the Ganges.

Throughout the sixth and seventh centuries one invasion followed the other. The intruders attempted to hold onto the region of India they had conquered and to establish permanent domination, but each failed in turn. The first invasion was that of the White Huns (Ephthalites) of Bactrian origin. This was followed by that of the Chalukyas (550-753), whose most famous king, Pulakēśin II (608-42), extended his rule to the south of

the peninsula, where numerous frescoes inspired by him are to be found. And lastly, in the south-eastern Deccan with their court at Kanchipuram, were the Pallavas, constant rivals of the Chalukyas, established at Badami. The Pallavas are known for encouraging Dravidian architecture.

This was an exceptional period, the equivalent of the European Middle Ages, when majestic cathedrals reaching towards heaven were built; there was an intense belief in Hinduism, a spiritual tidal-wave, the impetus of which was embodied in the construction of grandiose palaces and temples such as those in the princely towns of Aihole, Badami, Kanchipuram, Pattadakal and Mahābalipuram.

The Chalukyas, expelled in their turn, were succeeded by the Rāshtrakūtas in 753. The latter established themselves at Māhlked, which they made their capital. The Kailashanatha Temple at Ellora, an edifice without parallel, was built under the reign of one of their kings, Krishna I (757-83). But the Chalukyas would not admit defeat and, reorganized, their descendants ousted the Rāshtrakūta dynasty and regained power for a short while as a second Chalukya dynasty.

The sumptuous Buddhist Pāla dynasty controlled most of Bengal and Bihar from the eighth century to the twelfth. Among the multitude of small kingdoms that formed central India, one must mention that of the Pratiharas, ancestors of the celebrated Rajput clans, and that of the Chandellas who favoured Brahmanism and constructed a multitude of temples at Khajurāho. This period saw a renaissance of Hinduism, distinguished by a flowering of literature and philosophy. Schools of thought blossomed; their structures and powerful insight have succeeded in enriching Hindu thinking right to this day. The sage Shankarāchārya, or Shankara (788-838), constructed a religious philosophy derived from the essential values of Buddhism and from Hindu traditions. He undertook to define, on the one hand, man's place in the heart of the universe and, on the other, the presence of the Divine Absolute in each being. Shankara achieved fame as the interpreter of the *Vedanta* school and as the propagator of the non-dualist *Advaita* philosophy.

The Brahman philosopher Ramanuja (1050-1137) disagreed with Shankara's theory. He developed a new *Vaishnava* doctrine on the relations between man and God, the *Vishishtadvaita*, a mitigated non-dualism: whilst safeguarding the absolute character of the Divinity, Ramanuja stressed the personality of man and the identity of his soul that could not be destroyed by the Creator. For ten centuries these two doctrines have served as the basis of reflection for many thinkers obsessed by the mystery of the One and the Many, i.e. the Creator and created beings.

From the thirteenth century India was subjected to strong pressures from abroad. Her culture was threatened by Muslim influences manifested in buildings, mosques and minarets of Iranian style such as the Qutb-Minar and the Masjid-i-Quwwat-ul-Islam at Delhi. But India reacted and rediscovered her identity; her history from then on pursues a firmer course. Under Mughal reign from the sixteenth to the eighteenth century, Indian civilization was profoundly affected by Persia, and abundant traces remain at Agra, Delhi and Lahore. The Taj Mahal at Agra is indisputably the finest of the buildings resulting from this Persian influence.

The fearless and vital Mughal dynasty (1526-1857) reunited India. Babur (1483-1530), its founder, was a king on a grand scale. He was devoted to learning and to beauty, and it was through him that the art of the carpet was implanted in India. Although of Turkish origin, Babur was not content merely to write well in his native tongue. Steeped in Persian culture, he wrote poetry and recited his own verses in that language. He had a high regard for artists, encouraged their efforts and benefited from the stimulus of their talents.

Moreover, Babur was gifted with rare physical strength. At the age of eleven, he inherited the principality of Ferghana, a small kingdom east of Samarkand, from his father. His domain, although small, obliged him to engage in warfare with the Uzbeks, descendants of Timur (Tamerlane), covetous of the remains of the ancestral empire. Already as a young man, Babur had twice established himself on the throne of Samarkand, Tamerlane's capital, by his own hand. Then, overthrown and hunted, he lived for ten years as a nomad in camps and huts. For the fourth time, he succeeded in acquiring a throne, this time at Kabul (1504). With his power firmly consolidated, he threw himself into the conquest of India. Four successive campaigns ended in defeat, but he stubbornly resumed his onslaughts. Finally, the fifth led him to his objective, and Babur became master of India. In 1526, on the plain at Pānipat, Babur found himself face to face with the powerful army of the sultan of Delhi, one hundred thousand strong, reinforced with one hundred elephants. He defeated the Indians and shared out the vast wealth of the vanquished sultan among his officers and soldiers, keeping nothing for himself; such indifference to wealth won Babur the nickname of 'beggar-monk'. The only title to fame to which he attached any value, however, was that of 'Founder of the Indian Empire'.

Humayun (1530-56), who succeeded his father Babur, was a charming, clever and fascinating man. But a king must be tirelessly energetic and possess military skill, qualities Humayun lacked. With the complicity of a particularly cunning Afghan general, Sher Khan, his brothers betrayed him. Humayun was dethroned and found a lukewarm welcome in Persia at the court of Shah Tahmasp, who gave him the throne of Kabul in order to be rid of him. Humayun remained there for some years, and then in the course of a campaign succeeded in retaking Delhi, where he reigned for but a few months: Humayun died after falling down a marble staircase in his own palace. It was said of him, ironically, that he died in a manner befitting his life: for when he had occasion to fall, he did not fail to grasp it.

Akbar (1556-1605), son of Humayun, was a great Mughal emperor. Broad-minded politically, rather than unifying the country by force of arms he employed the more humane method of diplomacy. Akbar ended all discrimination between Hindu and Muslim, and it was during his reign that the weaving of hand-knotted carpets was begun: Akbar set up workshops commissioned to create rugs for his palace at Fatehpur, which was his showplace, and for his harem that housed more than five thousand women.

One cannot view these Mughal buildings without being moved by both admiration and sadness; for there exist traces of a grandiose dream, lost forever. The buildings are set upon a rocky hill-top, surrounded on three sides by walls 11 kilometres (6.8 miles) in length; the well-preserved royal palaces are entered by portals, each finer than its predecessor. The principal entrance, the Victory Gate, is certainly the most majestic anywhere in India.

Known today as Fatehpur Sikri, this site lies at a distance of 38 kilometres (23.6 miles) from Agra. In the village of Sikri not far from Fatehpur lived a Muslim sage, Shaikh Salim Chishti. One day in 1568, to consult on the subject of his descendants, Akbar decided to visit him: in 1562, the emperor had married a Rajput princess, Maryam Zamani, daughter of the Raja of Amber, none of whose boy children had survived, to the deep despair of her husband who longed for a male descendant. Salim Chishti predicted that Akbar would soon have a son to assure the succession, and the following year, when Maryam gave birth to the long-awaited heir, the Great Mughal Akbar, full of gratitude, named him Salim. This son was to become Emperor Jahangir. Historians question whether it was this happy event that decided Akbar to build his capital near the village of Salim Chishti or whether, quite simply, he wished to escape the sparse confines of the fort at Agra.

Be that as it may, Fatehpur Sikri was not destined to remain the royal residence for long; for in 1588, a mere fourteen years after completion, the court abandoned it. The reason for this is not known, perhaps lack of water or the whim of a favourite.

Akbar was a man of many talents, with highly developed and refined tastes. He was possessed of a creativity always receptive to new ideas. The flower-patterned carpets of silk or of the finest wool that he had made for Fatehpur are considered the most beautiful of the Mughal period, while the animal and bird rugs seem to be the work of his successors. Moreover, as a lively conversationalist, Akbar enjoyed the company of philosophers and scholars and indulged his passion for books in his amply stocked library. Endowed with a rare physical strength like his grandfather Babur, Akbar was fearless. In the hunt he would face the tiger and elephant squarely; while in battle, in the campaigns of the forty-nine years of his reign, he personally led his soldiers against hostile forces ten times greater in number. Akbar was cast in the same mould as David, whom the Psalms describe as the victor over ten thousand men.

Jahangir (1605-27), the son and successor of Akbar, was also a patron of the arts and writes in his Memoirs: 'So great was my love of painting that I could tell the name of the artist, whether living or dead, by looking at his work'. The wonders of nature impressed Jahangir deeply; he commissioned Mansur and Murad, two artists at his court, to paint the most beautiful animals, birds and plants, especially those native to Kashmir, which Jahangir called 'the Garden of Eternal Spring'. Therefore at his request Mansur painted no less than one hundred different flowers from that land of dreams.

According to Arthur Dilley (New York, 1959), it was under Jahangir that trade with the English was initiated, and huge sums of money were invested in the manufacture of carpets and the expansion of that industry. The effects of this financial endeavour were to endure until the beginning of the twentieth century.

The earliest commercial relations between India and Europe had been established through the intermediary of Arab and Egyptian traders who directed the merchandise they obtained in the Orient to Venice. From 1498 to 1580 the Portuguese monopolized trade with India, constructing heavy fortifications to guarantee the security of their traffic along the coastline. In 1600 the English created the first East India Company with a first factory (1611) at Masulipatnam on the Coromandel coast. The Dutch founded their own Dutch East India Company in 1602. Aided by the Dutch, the English ousted the Portuguese in 1606. And in 1664 the French followed with their own East India Company.

Jahangir's successor, Shah Jahan (1627-58), was the most beloved and majestic of the Great Mughals. His benevolence towards his people was that of a father towards his children; Shah Jahan was venerated rather than feared. François Bernier, a Frenchman who was the court physician, described the sumptuous beauty with which the audience chamber was filled on great occasions: the sovereign was enthroned at the end of the room, magnificently dressed in a tunic of white satin displaying delicate embroidery in gold thread, and with a turban of gold weave sporting an *aigrette* set with diamonds of huge dimensions and a topaz of a brilliance that rivalled the sun. His necklace of enormous pearls hung down to his stomach; his Peacock Throne was mounted upon four feet of solid gold and set with emeralds, rubies and diamonds. Shah Jahan had commissioned this throne in order to display the vast reserve of precious stones accumulated in the Treasury. And lastly, silk carpets covered every surface of the room.

The luxury with which Shah Jahan liked to surround himself also emanates from the buildings inspired by him.

The royal residence that he built in Delhi is one of the purest jewels ever conceived by man; and his Taj Mahal at Agra is considered, even today, to be one of the wonders of the world.

The brilliant and peaceful reign established by Shah Jahan was to be disturbed by his successor, Aurangzeb (1658-1707). The latter, a fanatical Muslim, wiped out Akbar's efforts to conciliate the Hindus. He persecuted them and destroyed their temples, but during twenty years of conflict never succeeded in humbling their rebellion in the south of the country. Aurangzeb was forced to take refuge in Delhi where the peoples of the north, whose support he had counted on, proved hostile. The physician Gamelli-Carreri, who was the camp doctor, described Aurangzeb as an old man with a white beard and cadaverous features relieved by his refined apparel, seated upon rich carpets and resting on gold-embroidered cushions.

Nadir Shah, King of Persia, after chasing the Afghans from his country, attacked India. He laid siege to Delhi in 1738 and took the remaining Mughals prisoner. With his assent, the Persian soldiers pillaged the city for two months; Nadir Shah carried off to Persia the fabulous Peacock Throne of Shah Jahan.

And so the Mughal Empire, harassed by Persian invasions, was shaken. In addition, a Hindu community of the Poona region (Maharashtra) arose in opposition and became autonomous in about 1680 under the aegis of Prince Sivaji Bhonsle. The Mahrathas became the most powerful force in the peninsula and enjoyed the support of many Hindus, who remembered the persecutions to which they had been subjected under Aurangzeb and saw in the redoubtable Mahratha warriors the instrument with which to revenge themselves on the Muslim tyranny of the Mughals.

Indian Carpets

Here we shall interrupt our survey of the history of India to take note of some events in the story of the carpet.

In his book (London, 1908), Sir G. Watt mentions that the Indian carpet was described under the name of *alcatif* (*katif* being the Arabic word for a pile carpet). Mention of carpets was made too by Pinto in 1540, by Tenreiro in 1560, by Linschoten in 1598 and by Pyrard who, in 1608, reminisces on Portuguese ladies of Goa seated upon precious *alcatifs*.

One of the first carpets from the imperial looms at Lahore that is known to us is that presented in 1634 to the Girdlers' Company in London by Robert Bell, Master of the Girdlers' Company and a director of the East India Company; it is reproduced on page 72 of this work. In the opinion of Arthur Dilley, the Mughal carpets, which are among the most splendid creations of the seventeenth century, were woven in the reigns of Akbar, Jahangir and Shah Jahan at Agra, Fatehpur, Lahore and Delhi. Examples are in the collections of the Central Museum and the City Palace of Jaipur; the Österreichisches Museum für angewandte Kunst, Vienna; the Victoria and Albert Museum, London; the Metropolitan Museum of Art, New York; the Textile Museum, Washington, D.C. and the Museum of Fine Arts, Boston. The Girdlers' Carpet, which bears the coats-of-arms of both Bell and the

Girdlers' Company, as well as Bell's monogram, is now in a place of honour in the Company's Hall in London.

The weavers of floral carpets in India were of Persian origin, and thus the Persian influence is evident in their art. The Mughal prayer rugs, however, are of typically Indian style. Indian carpets of this period are distinguished from Persian carpets by their colouring, which differs from the Persian palette in lightness and clarity, in the pink used to outline the motifs and in the incomparable fineness of the knotting. The fragment of the silk rug in the Altmann Collection at the Metropolitan Museum of Art in New York has a knot-count of just over 3,900,000 per square metre (2,516 per square inch). Such carpets with silk warp, weft and pile must have been woven under Shah Jahan, contemporary with his building of the Taj Mahal.

Unfortunately, after the fall of the Mughals, the East India companies encouraged the production of carpets that would be commercially viable in Europe; they were not as sumptuous and produced with less care.

In India, as in the Middle East, only scant information is available on knotted carpets made between the seventeenth and the nineteenth centuries. Production must have been somewhat sparse, since there exist only a few rare examples from the eighteenth century.

It was in the nineteenth century, when trade with Europe intensified, that the carpet industry enjoyed a revival in India. The Crystal Palace Exhibition in London in 1851, at which several Indian carpets were exhibited, brought that country to the attention of dealers who were not slow to realize the possibilities of increasing financial profit by shifting their source of production from Turkey and Persia to India; however, through their exploitation, they were to be instrumental in causing a deterioration of standards.

Carpet-producing Centres

Two exceptionally beautiful Kashmiri knotted carpets of the seventeenth century, in typically Indian style, caused a stir at the Crystal Palace Exhibition.

At the beginning of this century, Amritsar was the most important Indian centre of carpet knotting, while Agra, alongside its local production, was engaged essentially in distribution. In Uttar Pradesh, Mirzapur concentrated on manufacturing cheap rugs from designs provided by European and American companies. It is superfluous to comment that the reputation of the Indian carpet suffered as a result of this overly commercial approach.

Rugs of a typically Indian style are still produced in the province of Maharashtra in the small town of Ellora, well known for its tourist attractions.

Mahābalipuram, another tourist centre lying to the south of Madras, is the oldest centre of the carpet industry in India. Four Persian families of carpet weavers settled there some time before 1550. Their work excited such admiration that one director of the East India Company wrote: 'The carpets woven in this town, in the Persian manner, are truly the most beautiful. In addition, the town is a thriving port which serves as a meeting point for Chinese, English, Dutch, Portuguese, French and Persians, all concerned with trade'.

Warangal in the province of Andhra Pradesh is reputed for the beauty of its temples, the quality of its wool and for some very fine carpets, the most famous of which, dating from the sixteenth century, is now in London. Others were exhibited at Jaipur in 1883.

H.T. Harris mentioned other centres of the carpet industry in his *Monograph on the Carpet Weaving Industry of Southern India* (1908): Waljapet, Bangalore, Tanjore and Malabar.

Although Ahmedabad is frequently described as a carpet-manufacturing town, by the beginning of this century only some small factories survived there.

Let us conclude by listing the major centres still producing the knotted carpets that excite our untiring admiration: Uttar Pradesh (Agra, Bhadohi and Mirzapur), Kashmir, the Punjab (Amritsar), Madhya Pradesh (Gwalior) and Rajasthan (Jaipur).

TECHNICAL SURVEY

Materials

From the outset—in India, as in other countries—wool has always been the basic material of the knotted carpet. The role of camel's and goat's hair is almost negligible; however, in Kashmir especially, silk is commonly used not only for the pile but also for the warp and weft, particularly in the case of a high-quality piece.

The wool used for the pile has a variety of origins, the choice depending upon the role for which the carpet is intended. For an average-quality rug the local product is mixed with imported wool, provided the latter is neither too thin nor too dry. But when prize pieces are being produced, only lustrous wools are used, supplied from regions specializing in their preparation. This problem does not exist in Kashmir, where the weaver has at his command a wool that surpasses all others in quality.

Normally the warp and the weft are of cotton. Attempts have been made to replace cotton with jute in inferior-quality rugs, but because of its poor resistance to wear, the use of jute has been abandoned.

At the beginning of this century, wool for rugs was still most commonly coloured by means of natural dyes. Madder, which grows wild almost everywhere, was the most important colorant of vegetable origin. Its root provides the whole range of pinks and reds that can also be extracted from cochineal and turmeric. A very pure yellow is derived from the stigma of the cultivated saffron crocus, widely grown in Kashmir, and a reddish-yellow is derived from its wild counterpart. A light yellow is provided by the distillation of the turmeric root, and another shade of yellow from pomegranate skins. According to C. Latimer, dark red and copper-red are obtained from rhubarb. Green is derived from grass (*kuśà*) and brown from the leaves of the *kikar* tree.

Nowadays, in India as elswhere, synthetic dyes are in general use, which is regrettable; for when one contemplates an early carpet, the pile is brought to life with an interplay of infinite reflections—it is impossible to achieve such an alluring sheen with chemically dyed wool. In addition the natural dyes were studiously prepared in the craftsmen's own homes, while the synthetic products come from manufacturers or professional dyers.

Dyeing

The peoples of Asia are the undisputed masters of the art of dyeing. They manage to achieve luminous tones, warm and sober at the same time, that animate their work while imbuing the carpets with incredible subtlety. It is hard to imagine colours more fascinating than those of the carpets and textiles of India.

Patterns

Pattern is just as much an integral part of the knotted carpet as colouring, and both are elements of primary importance.

In order to understand the present state of the carpet-making industry in the East, it must be remembered that for 2,500 years the only patterns reproduced, in varying degrees of stylization, were those of flowers, arabesques and rhomboids, with an occasional animal design. These patterns have never become outmoded, while designs of modern or Western inspiration have not succeeded in establishing themselves. The majority of oriental motifs have a profound meaning: the circle signifies eternity, the zigzag water and light, the swastika a light showing the way in darkness, the meander the continuity of life and the tree happiness or goodness. A traditional pattern is usually composed of a choice of motifs from among roses, lotus, poppies, myrtle, henna, crocus, narcissus, lilies, the tree-of-life and a variety of birds.

The newly revived carpet industry in India had to follow the traditional oriental style to compete in the market. Classical designs, almost all of Persian provenance, were adopted; nevertheless, some patterns in common usage were of Indian or Chinese origin. As a result of painstaking and lengthy experiments deriving their inspiration from sixteenth- and seventeenth-century Indian examples and early Indian textiles, the country has succeeded in making an impact upon traditional patterns. While Persian weavers prefer to depict animals such as lions or tigers, Indian weavers would rather represent birds. There is also a difference between the Persian and the Indian manner of depicting flowers.

The usual procedure adopted by a carpet-designer is as follows: having drawn up his design, he transfers it to graph paper on which each square represents a single knot. Then he divides the paper into varying sizes, depending on whether the pattern is intended for the central medallion or for a part of a repeat pattern. These sheets of paper are then passed to the knotting workshop.

In Kashmir and at Amritsar, there is a special manner of transmitting the pattern to the weavers: a coded colour-chart (*talim*), a procedure that the weavers of Kashmir had used when making shawls, since the cartoon was unknown to them. Converted to carpet-knotting, Kashmiri weavers did not wish to change their practices, so they adapted the *talim* to carpet weaving. When the carpet industry was revived at Amritsar in the last century, the *talim* became common in the ateliers of the region because the weavers came from Kashmir. The *talim* is a roll of paper marked with a code indicating the number of knots to be woven in their respective colours. The master-weaver reads aloud from it, and the knotters follow his directions carefully. On the *talim* colours are designated by the following signs:

ꝺ = green (*zangari*)
ö = white (*chot*)
ꝺ = pink (*gulabi*)
o̲ = yellow (*zard*)
o̒ = garnet (*anari*), and so on.

The number of knots to be woven is also indicated by signs, for example:

ꝺo = 20 knots in green.

20

1

2

3

4

Preparation of a *talim* demands time and experience; the person entrusted with the task refers to a traditional cartoon traced by a designer. This cartoon is divided into squares of twenty-five compartments, five from top to bottom and five across. Each compartment represents one knot that is marked onto the *talim*, which is a roll of paper in this case. On completion of the cartoon, the designer's next step is to select the colours that will bring the design to life, and to attach samples to a chart, matching each colour with the *talim* code. When all these elements are assembled, the *talim* can finally be written out. This is a lengthy chore: for a carpet measuring 300×200 centimetres (118×79 inches), with a knot-count of 570,000 per square metre (368 per square inch)—quite common in Kashmir— two hundred strips of paper will be used for a design with a central medallion and eight hundred strips for a continuous pattern. Where there is a central medallion, it is only necessary for a quarter of the design to be drawn out and transposed three times. Once the *talim* is complete, it is passed on (together with the cartoon and colour chart) to the master-weaver who winds the warp around the loom. Then the master-weaver begins chanting the *talim*, and the knotters chant their reply ('*hau*'), meaning that they have carried out their instructions.

Roller-beam loom   *Simple village loom*

Looms and Knots

The roller-beam loom is the one most commonly used in India. The simplest of these looms are composed of two horizontal wooden beams between which the warp threads are stretched: one beam in front of the weaver, the second beam behind the first. As the knotting proceeds, the carpet is rolled to the back of the loom.

To make a carpet, the weaver begins by weaving a selvedge: several shoots of weft are passed to form a narrow band—a sort of coarse cloth—intended to secure the knots at the end of the carpet (this process will be repeated at the opposite end on completion of the weaving).

The asymmetrical (or Persian) knot is used almost exclusively in India. This knot is tied with a strand of yarn around two adjacent warp threads, leaving some warp threads free at either side for the lateral selvedges. However, unlike the symmetrical (or Turkish) knot, in the asymmetrical knot the strand of yarn being tied encircles only one warp thread while simply passing behind the other. In this way, the two ends of the yarn appear separately at different places: the first between the two adjacent warp threads mentioned, and the second between one of these and the next warp thread. Each knot is separated from its neighbour by a loop that is cut after

the next shoot of weft. This asymmetrical knot can be executed just as easily from right to left as from left to right, which is why it is also sometimes called the 'two-handed knot'. The knot can also be tied around four warp threads by taking up two at a time. This practice is becoming increasingly widespread, for in this way knotting progresses more rapidly, but the resulting carpet is weaker in structure.

In Kashmir this method is termed the 'double knot', which can be misleading. In some countries the same term is used to describe a knotting process in which half of the knot's 'hump' lies above the other half as a result of the tension of the weft threads, which are picked up in alternate sets of two as they pass through the warp. This manner of weaving undoubtedly increases the number of knots and produces carpets of enhanced solidity. In English-speaking countries, this method of knotting is known as the 'depressed warp'.

Knot tied around two warp threads

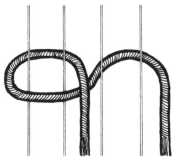

Knot tied around four warp threads

5 *Woollen yarn of different colours,* talim *and cartoon used* ▷
   to prepare the talim
6 *Final shearing of the pile*
7 *Washing a carpet*

5

6

8

CARPET-PRODUCING REGIONS

Kashmir

In the third century BC Emperor Asoka sent Buddhist missionaries to Kashmir, where they founded Srinagar, the first town to be built in that country. The historian Kalhana enumerates a long succession of fifty-two kings from Asoka up to Kanishka, who died in AD 144.

After the White Huns (Ephthalites) led by Mihiragula had passed through, the Karkota dynasty restored Hinduism to its privileged position in Kashmir. This return to the ancestral faith was celebrated by the construction of new temples. In 1338, the Hindu ruler Udiana Deva was put to death by the Muslim grand vizier, Amir Shah, who ascended the throne as Shams-ud-Din; and so, once again, Kashmir was delivered up to Islam. In 1398, when India was being invaded by Timur (Tamerlane), Sultan Sikandar, father of Shahi Kan, sent his son to pay tribute to the invader. But instead of sealing the alliance agreed with Sultan Sikandar, Timur betrayed his promise and kept Sikandar's son as a hostage.

The young prince remained in Samarkand for seven years, whither Timur had earlier transported the finest artists and craftsmen from the countries under his sway, none of whom was free to leave the city without authorization. Prince Shahi Kan, at liberty to move about as he wished, was greatly impressed by the talents of all these workers; therefore, when he was able to return to Kashmir, he invited some of them to accompany him.

On the death of his father Sikandar, whom he succeeded under the title of Zain-ul-Abadin, he set to work with alacrity. First, he introduced the culture of the mulberry tree and the silkworm. Then he established the embroidery and *papier-mâché* trades imported from China. Next, Zain-ul-Abadin sent emissaries to Persia, central Asia and Arabia to seek out and enlist craftsmen of every calling, in particular those skilled in the making of knotted carpets. So greatly did he contribute to the prosperity and renown of his people that Zain-ul-Abadin is considered the precursor of the Mughals, the Akbar of Kashmir.

It is possible that the art of carpet-knotting in Kashmir preceded Zain-ul-Abadin's reign, but no written evidence of this exists, nor are any rugs known to us from an earlier date.

Later, in the seventeenth century at the time when Ahmed Beg Khan was appointed by Shah Jahangir to govern Kashmir (1615-18), the merchant Akhun Rahnuma became involved in carpet manufacture. He had travelled to Mecca on the *Hajj* (pilgrimage) and, on his return, breaking his journey in Persia, he learned the craft of carpet-knotting. Struck by the notion of introducing the industry into Kashmir, Akhun returned with the necessary equipment and trained some weavers. Production began, but with only fleeting success, since the Kashmiri textile workers preferred to make shawls.

It was not until the nineteenth century that carpet-making was really revived in Kashmir. As in other regions of the Middle East, its growth depended upon demand from the West. In about 1876 a certain Mr Chapman journeyed to Kashmir intending to relaunch

◁ 8 *Srinagar*

31

the manufacture of rugs. This undertaking was not without its difficulties, and only after several years of effort did he arrive at a stage where the product began to be known in overseas markets. But Chapman's perseverance was eventually rewarded: Kashmiri rugs were awarded medals at various international exhibitions—Chicago (1893), Delhi (1903), London (1906).

During the nineteenth century, the market for cashmere shawls was dwindling in Europe as a result of the introduction of mechanical weaving. From then on many Kashmiri craftsmen transferred their skills from shawls to carpet-making. Already acquainted with the most delicate work, they quickly developed expertise for the most minute knotting. Rather than employ the carpet-knotter's usual cartoon (a squared drawing) for the design of the motifs, they followed the method they had used to make the patterns on shawls: a *talim* (see pages 20, 25).

It is hardly surprising that a country renowned throughout the world for the fineness of its wool should also be famed for the quality of its carpets, and Kashmiri carpets are indeed second to none. Today, Kashmir is concentrating on achieving a typically local character for its rugs. A government-sponsored school at Srinagar teaches the use of designs based on ancestral Kashmiri motifs, which are already being reproduced sucessfully by some craft workshops.

Kashmir is famous not only for carpets but also for wood-carvings, *repoussé* copper metalwork, objects of painted *papier-mâché* and especially for garments made from the matchless indigenous wool.

Tradition has it that the valley of Kashmir was covered in the past by *Satisara*, 'Sea of Sati' (Śiva's wife). Then the gods, granting the prayers of the ascetic Kashyapa, whose zeal impressed them, caused the lake to dry up. Thus the name Kashmir supposedly derives from *Kashmira*, 'Lake of Kashyapa'.

The heart of Kashmir, the Vale of Kashmir, as the valley of the River Jhelum is termed, is perhaps the most beautiful landscape in the whole of India. Each year, countless tourists come to admire the lakes, floating houses and Mughal gardens there, including the Shalimar Gardens ('Refuge of Love'), and the temples at Pahalgam and Gulmarg.

The Punjab

Amritsar, the spiritual home of the Sikh religion, is the principal city and most important industrial and commercial centre of the Punjab, with a population of more than half a million.

The name Amritsar, or Amrita Sagar, means 'Lake of Immortality'. The city was founded in 1577 by the fourth Sikh guru, Ram Das, and since that time his shrine, the Golden Temple, has remained the spiritual axis of Sikhism. This elegant construction of white marble

 9 *Srinagar, Dal Lake* ▷
10 *On a canal in Srinagar*
11 *Srinagar, a house-boat*
12 *On a canal in Srinagar*
13 *Mughal gardens in Srinagar*

13

15

embellished with gold and silver is set in an ornamental lake surrounded by white edifices that shelter the numerous pilgrims from far and wide, and serve to insulate the Golden Temple from the noises of the city. There are many other religious buildings in Amritsar, since the population is by no means uniquely Sikh.

Right in the centre of Amritsar is the Jallianwala Bagh ('Garden of the Flame of Liberty'), where a monument of red sandstone commemorates the sad day of 13 April 1919, when the English General Dyer gave the order to fire upon a crowd of peaceful demonstrators appealing for independence; three hundred and seventy-nine were killed and twelve hundred wounded. The scars of the bullets can still be seen on the walls enclosing the garden. The shooting was followed by a fierce repression, which served to awaken the Indian national conscience.

To the north of Amritsar, opposite the Rambagh Gate, are the Rambagh Gardens laid out by Ranjit Singh, who erected a pavilion there, where he delighted in passing quiet moments.

The earliest seventeenth-century carpets, from the reign of Akbar, were made at Lahore, in the Pakistani Punjab, where a manufactory was established that prospered until the end of the eighteenth century.

From 1809 an important development occurred in the carpet industry. Maharaja Ranjit Singh encouraged the recruitment of shawl-weavers from Kashmir, and eventually many settled in Amritsar because the shawl industry in their own area was declining, since it was penalized by overly onerous taxes at a time when Western demand was diminishing. These immigrants from Kashmir, already trained craftsmen, provided an ideal labour force for the launching of the Punjabi carpet industry.

The first factories which opened at Amritsar c. 1860 used Bokhara patterns. However, the Kashmiri weavers retained their own techniques and used the *talim* for knotting, in place of a cartoon. Thus Amritsar became the second Indian centre to use the *talim*, or coded pattern-guide, for the knotting of carpets.

Agra

Situated at a distance of some 200 kilometres (124 miles) from Delhi, Agra, the fourth town of the province Uttar Pradesh, was probably a frontier post at the time when the Yamuna River constituted the southern limit of Aryan territory. The *Mahābhārata* describes events traditionally held to have taken place c. 3000 BC; the surviving version, which dates from the first half of the first millennium AD, mentions the town under the name of Agrabana, which may signify 'Paradise' in the archaic Sanskrit of the time. Agra's significance in classical times was well attested by Ptolemy of Alexandria, who called it Agara.

The real renown of Agra dates from the sixteenth century. In 1504 Sikandar Lodi chose it as capital of his states. In 1526 Agra was captured by Babur, and later

14   *Amritsar, the Golden Temple with its ornamental lake*
15   *Amritsar, the Golden Temple*
◁16   *Agra, the Taj Mahal*

41

under Akbar's reign (1556-1605), it became the capital of the Mughal Empire, although from 1574 to 1588 the Mughal court resided primarily at Fatehpur Sikri. Akbar died at Agra in 1605. It was probably during his reign that the production of knotted carpets was initiated at Agra. Akbar had established a carpet manufactory at Lahore, and as early as 1619 carpet workshops were being mentioned at Agra.

Under Jahangir (1605-27) Agra remained the Mughal capital. In 1612 at Agra the emperor granted a *firman* ('official letter or proclamation') for the first time to the representatives of the British East India Company, giving them licence to trade in India.

Jahangir died in 1627 and was succeeded by his son Khurram, who took the name of Shah Jahan ('King of the World'). Arjumand Bano Begam, whom he married in 1612, became Mumtaz-i Mahal ('Chosen of the Palace'). This title seems to have been merited, for Mumtaz-i Mahal was so extraordinarily beautiful, and Shah Jahan so enamoured of her, that while she lived it is said that he had eyes for no other woman. In 1631 Mumtaz-i Mahal died at the age of thirty-seven, and already by 1632 construction of her mausoleum had begun—the Taj Mahal, one of the wonders of the world.

All superlatives have long since been exhausted in describing the Taj Mahal. François Bernier, who saw it in 1663, declared: 'This is a tomb that deserves to rank among the marvels of this world more than the crude masses of stones in Egypt'. Although building of the Taj Mahal began in 1632, it took eleven years to complete this monumental complex, which contains two lateral mosques (one is an assembly hall), a portal and a garden.

At the Red Fort in Agra the sovereign had constructed several buildings: the Khas Mahal ('Private Apartments'), the Diwan-i Khas ('Private Audience Hall'), the Shish Mahal ('Palace of Mirrors') and the Diwan-i Amm ('General Audience Hall'). In 1658, Aurangzeb imprisoned his father, Shah Jahan, and his sister, Begam Saheb, in the Red Fort at Agra, from where Shah Jahan could gaze across the Yamuna River at the Taj Mahal.

Agra was sacked in 1761 by the Jats of Bharatpur and was occupied for a while by the Marathas of Gwalior in 1764. In 1803 it formed part of the possessions of the British East India Company, and finally, in 1863, Agra was granted municipal status.

The manufacture of carpets, which had reached its peak of splendour under the Mughals, declined after their dynasty fell. Only a few workshops continued making carpets to satisfy regional demand. During the second quarter of the nineteenth century, a German company reorganized the carpet industry at Agra for the purpose of export, but with little result.

In 1947, with the independence and partition of India and Pakistan, many Muslim artisans emigrated to Pakistan. But since then the work-force has been restored

17   *A pavilion of the Taj Mahal* ▷
18   *Side view of the Taj Mahal*
19   *A close-up of a monumental niche in the Taj Mahal*
20   *Agra, the Taj Mahal: detail of a low relief*
21   *Agra, the Taj Mahal: enlarged detail of a flower in the preceding low relief*

◁ 18
19 ▷

23

to strength, and Agra is now possessed of an excellent knotted-carpet industry.

One peculiarity of the weaving process at Agra is the *phera bolna*, or reading aloud of the pattern. The master-weaver alone sees the design, and he dictates the colour to be knotted to each weaver in a special language: sky-blue is called *mithi*, dark blue *gahri*, mid-blue *surmai*. This might appear complicated, but in practice the method is quite easy to follow.

Jaipur

Although the city of Jaipur is relatively modern, it nevertheless attracts many tourists. There are magnificent palaces, in particular the City Palace, former residence of the Maharaja whose descendants still live in part of the building. The rest of the palace, arranged as a museum, is open to the public and contains, among other wonderful objects, a very fine collection of early carpets.

Previously, since the twelfth century, the sovereigns had resided at Amber, not far from the present-day city, whose old town is a popular tourist attraction. Situated at a distance of 8 kilometres (4.9 miles) from Jaipur in the direction of Delhi, Amber is built among a circle of towering hills crowned with forts and watch-towers. In 1727, Jai Singh II abandoned Amber for the plain and

founded present-day Jaipur, which he made his capital. The advent of manufacturers, jewellers and bankers from Delhi and Agra quickly brought affluence to the city.

Jaipur was the first city in northern India to be built according to a plan. The Jantar Mantar Observatory near the City Palace is the best-preserved of five such observatories throughout the country. (The others are to be found in Delhi, Benares [Varanasi], Mathura and Ujjain.) It functioned for time-keeping purposes until 1940, for until that year Jaipur did not keep time in the same way as the rest of the country. One especially interesting structure in Jaipur is the Hawa Mahal ('Palace of the Winds'), which is nothing more than a façade pierced by many windows. It is not known why this astonishing palace was built in 1799. Its owner, Maharaja Sawai Pratap Singh, was a poet with a deep devotion to the god Krishna and the goddess Rādhā; in a couplet attributed to him, the building is dedicated to these two divinities. Another, more romantic explanation hints that the building served as a pavilion for the women of the royal harem, permitting them to watch the happenings of the city unobserved.

The tradition of craftsmanship is as old as the city of Jaipur itself. Maharaja Man Singh I, creator of the Amber Palace, attracted the first artisans—enamellers whose skill was highly esteemed—and other craftsmen to his palace. When present-day Jaipur had been built, they were induced to settle there with their families. The art of enamelling on gold and silver is still practised in Jaipur today. Fabrics, hand-printed with wooden blocks, and pottery with a blue glaze derived from cobalt oxide are also a speciality of the city.

22   *Agra, the Red Fort*
23   *Lattice window in a Mughal palace*
◁ 24   *Jaipur, the Hawa Mahal ('Palace of the Winds')*

The carpet industry in Jaipur, though comparatively young, is developing rapidly, and manufacturers are seriously concerned with improving rug quality: rugs from Jaipur now rival in fineness and finish those from the most highly regarded regions.

The outskirts of Jaipur are dotted with remarkable buildings. Towards Amber there is the Jal Mahal ('Water' or 'Summer Palace') in Indo-Muslim style; and towards Galta, the Palace of Maharani Shishodia, princess of Mewar. She was the favourite wife of Jai Singh II and mother of Madho Singh I, who was born in her palace and reigned there from 1750 to 1767.

Near Galta are two important temples built by followers of Ramanuja, the celebrated Vaishnavite whose philosophy, mentioned earlier, developed the theory that spirit and matter are not to be considered as absolutely inseparable.

Upon a ridge stands the temple dedicated to the sun-god Surya. Each year at the spring equinox, to commemorate the descent to earth of the Kachwaha, progeny of the sun, Surya's statue is carried through Jaipur on a chariot drawn by white horses.

The Region of Benares

Legend has it that the city of Benares (now called Varanasi) was created by the god Vishnu; today it is a place of pilgrimage.

Benares is one of the oldest cities in the world, and its history extends over a period of more than four thousand years. Some historians believe that it was already famous when Rome was still unknown, when Greece was just becoming established and when Nebuchadnezzar attempted his assault on Jerusalem. Before it was annexed by Kosala, a small kingdom, called Kāsī or Benares, existed there.

The earliest written evidence concerning Benares dates from the second millennium BC and describes a flourishing city before the country was invaded by the Aryans, who followed the course of the Ganges downstream. Descriptions of the power and renown of Benares also abound in Sanskrit literature.

It was in the reign of the Mughal king Akbar that the finest temples of Benares were built. But his grandson, Shah Jahan, who would build the Taj Mahal, had all the temples under construction demolished—seventy-six in all.

Shah Jahan encouraged the thriving textile industry; however, the same could not be said for his son Aurangzeb, whose policies in favour of Islam created many enemies. The latter sought to prevent the Hindus from prospering, imposing a special tax on them and destroying their temples and cultural institutions. In 1659 Aurangzeb went so far as to destroy the temple of Krittivaseshavar in order to build the 'Alamgir Mosque with the same stones. Furthermore, he changed the name

25 *Jaipur, the City Palace* ▷
26 *Jaipur, the Jantar Mantar Observatory*
27 *A corner pavilion of the Jantar Mantar Observatory*

30

of Benares, renaming it Muhammabad, under which name it continued to be known, though only on official papers, until his death. Aurangzeb's cruel religious intransigence has never been forgotten in Benares.

Today, Benares is an important city that derives its renown primarily from its religious character, since it has always been the centre of Hinduism. A multitude of pilgrims is attracted to its site on the banks of the Ganges, which is believed to spring from a heavenly source and whose water is said to purify the soul of sins. These Hindu pilgrims undertake lengthy journeys in order to be able to pray in the holy city and to bathe in the holy water. The spectacle of this crowd washing in the Ganges at sunrise is deeply moving.

Since time immemorial, Benares has been known for its textile industry too. A treatise on the socio-economic administration of the Maurya dynasty in the third century BC is full of references concerning the silk and cotton production of Benares. Today it is the scarves and *saris* of silk, with interwoven gold and silver threads, that are the most familiar.

The true regional centre of the carpet trade is the small town of Bhadohi, close to Benares. Since its beginning in the eighteenth century, this industry has progressed steadily and has greatly expanded. The origin of carpet-weaving there is attributed to the misfortune of a Persian artisan: when the caravan in which he was travelling was attacked by brigands who robbed the party, almost all the members of the caravan were killed; he was lucky enough to escape the massacre and was warmly welcomed by the villagers of Bhadohi, where he settled. In return, he taught the villagers the craft of carpet-knotting. Today there are thirty thousand looms in this area, each requiring three weavers to function at peak efficiency.

In the nineteenth and early twentieth centuries, the carpets of nearby Mirzapur were highly prized, but today the production there is smaller than at Bhadohi, although a fair number of looms are still functioning.

28   *Benares seen from the Ganges*
29   *Benares, Hindu pilgrims bathing in the Ganges*
◁30   *Benares, close-up of Hindus bathing in the Ganges*

THE CARPETS: PLATES AND NOTES

MUGHAL CARPET FROM THE IMPERIAL WORKSHOPS (detail)

Date: 1625
National Gallery of Art, Washington, D.C.
(Widener Collection: C-328)
Dimensions: 404×191 cm (159×75 in)
Asymmetrical knot:
368,500 knots per sq. metre (238 per sq. inch)
*   67 knots per 10 cm length (17 per inch length)*
*   55 knots per 10 cm width (14 per inch width)*
Warp of 8 strands of undyed cotton
Weft of 3 strands of pink cotton
Wool pile

The detail reproduced opposite is from a so-called animal carpet made in the imperial Mughal factory, where compositions of native flowers or jungle scenes were woven. Another section of this carpet is shown on the following page.

Artists took their subjects from Mughal miniatures. Alongside real animals are fabulous beasts drawn from mythological accounts. The exuberance these animals express, such as the leopard pursuing the antelope, imbues the carpets with great activity and fills them with harmonious movement. The carpet-weavers also demonstrated great ingenuity by including in their designs animals with wings or human heads leaping through palmettes, flowers and foliage representing, in very elaborate form and rich colouring, the vegetation of the jungle. All of the motifs arrayed on the field are set off by the brilliant red ground.

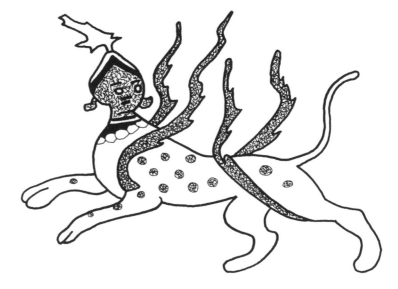

MUGHAL CARPET FROM THE IMPERIAL WORKSHOPS (detail)

Date: 1625
National Gallery of Art, Washington, D.C.
(Widener Collection: C-328)
Dimensions: 404×191 cm (159×75 in)
Asymmetrical knot:
368,500 knots per sq. metre (238 per sq. inch)
*   67 knots per 10 cm length (17 per inch length)*
*   55 knots per 10 cm width (14 per inch width)*
Warp of 8 strands of undyed cotton
Weft of 3 strands of pink cotton
Wool pile

Designs of the Mughal period depicting scenes of daily life, of which this piece is an example, display much charm. This was also true of the Mughal miniatures from which the creators of these carpets often derived their inspiration.

It would be an anomaly indeed if, in a collection of Indian carpets, no elephant ever appeared in the design, for over the centuries this noble beast has come to occupy a place of its own in Indian life.

Smaller than the African elephant and darker of skin, the Indian elephant as a domestic animal put its strength to use in many types of work, especially in forests for uprooting and dispatching timber. The elephant was also enlisted into the army to transport men and their baggage. And lastly, kings, princes and wealthy landowners used the elephant as a prestigious mount.

The great stature of a sumptuously caparisoned elephant inevitably lent importance to the person carried, as we see on this carpet. The man, clasping his crop, is conscious of his dignity; it seems natural that as he passes he frightens timid antelopes. Palms, flowers and foliage sway and dance about him, seeming to acknowledge his passage.

FRAGMENT OF A MUGHAL CARPET

Date: first half of the 17th century
Textile Museum, Washington, D.C. (R. 63.00.13)
Dimensions: 88×82 cm (35×32 in)
Asymmetrical knot:
325,500 knots per sq. metre (210 per sq. inch)
Cotton warp
Cotton weft
Wool pile

The Indian taste for the beauties of nature and inclination to depict scenes of daily life was already apparent in the miniatures that preceded this carpet in time and inspired its design.

Flowers and birds take first place in Indian taste, because of their great charm and exotic colouring, but scenes of jungle life are also frequently shown; hunting scenes in which man himself is seen to enjoy tracking down the animals are of Persian origin and only rarely adopted by the Indian workshops.

Fidelity to nature excluded neither experimentation nor fantasy, as the fragment opposite proves. Two men, who appear rather small perched upon huge elephants, engage in a rather unaggressive combat, despite the arms they carry and the confrontation of their mounts. The background decoration too is of a peaceful nature, with flowers and foliage in gold, red and black, and among it a wading bird watching the fight, not in the least startled. The red ground of the carpet imparts warmth to the scene in a manner typical of the creation of Indian weavers.

MUGHAL PICTORIAL CARPET (detail)

Date: late 16th or early 17th century
Museum of Fine Arts, Boston (Gift of Mrs Frederick L. Ames: 93.1480)
Dimensions: 243×154 cm (95.6×60.6 in)
Asymmetrical knot:
639,100 knots per sq. metre (412 per sq. inch)
   83 knots per 10 cm length (21 per inch length)
   77 knots per 10 cm width (20 per inch width)
Warp of undyed cotton
Weft of reddish-brown cotton
Pile of 2, 3 and 4 strands of wool

The plate opposite shows more than half of the field of a Mughal pictorial carpet, depicting a jungle scene and featuring legendary monsters alongside the customary animals.

Towards the bottom of this fragment is a fabulous beast with a slender body, an exceedingly long tail, winged chest and the head of an elephant with tusks and upturned trunk. In its claws, the monster grasps a young elephant, while it is being attacked itself by a phoenix that is putting out its eyes.

In the centre of the design, a man, whip in hand, passes through the jungle in a chariot drawn by two bulls. He is more likely to be a landowner returning from his estates than a warrior or a merchant. He is preceded by a servant bearing an antelope on his shoulders, a wounded animal or possibly a hunting trophy. Behind follows another servant, sabre in hand, watchful that the little convoy does not suffer a surprise attack. On the chariot, a tame leopard, held by a lead and with its paws planted squarely, mounts guard vigilantly behind its master, ready to ward off the assault of the lion that is turning its head menacingly towards them. Finally, right at the top, a panther attacks a white bull, which attempts in vain to disengage itself, while an antelope flees.

Such scenes are so numerous on carpets, and at times so similar, that it is difficult to state with certainty whether they are derived from legends or mythology.

FRAGMENT OF A MUGHAL ANIMAL CARPET

Date: late 16th — early 17th century
Glasgow Museums and Art Galleries: Burrell Collection,
Glasgow
Dimensions: 266×269 cm (105×106 in)
Asymmetrical knot:
60,000 knots per sq. metre (39 per sq. inch)
Cotton warp and weft
Wool pile

Controversy still surrounds the dating of the appearance of the iconography that inspired patterns such as the one on this carpet fragment, which distort nature yet maintain an enigmatic quality.

The patterns of this fragment are not dissimilar to those on vase carpets, with heads taking the place of vases. The motifs are really nothing more than heads with long necks, the bodies being merely a sort of long tail intended to anchor one motif to the others. Lions, tigers, bulls, elephants, horses, serpents, eagles, ibexes and rabbits are all in evidence. Some hold others in their jaws or in their grip, for instance the eagle carrying some small beast in each claw of its talons, shaped like a bird's beak. This tangle of motifs, between which small bunches of flowers creep, leaves no space for a central medallion.

The style of these images is reminiscent of the miniatures that illustrated pre-seventeenth-century manuscripts. They also appear on the carpet fragments in collections in the Louvre and in Washington, D.C. and were probably inspired by early legends.

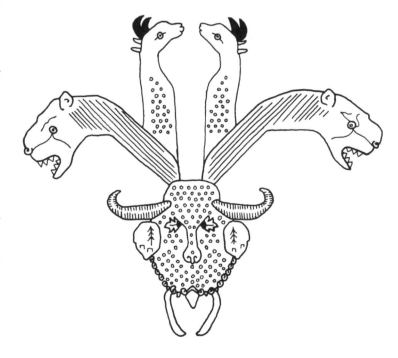

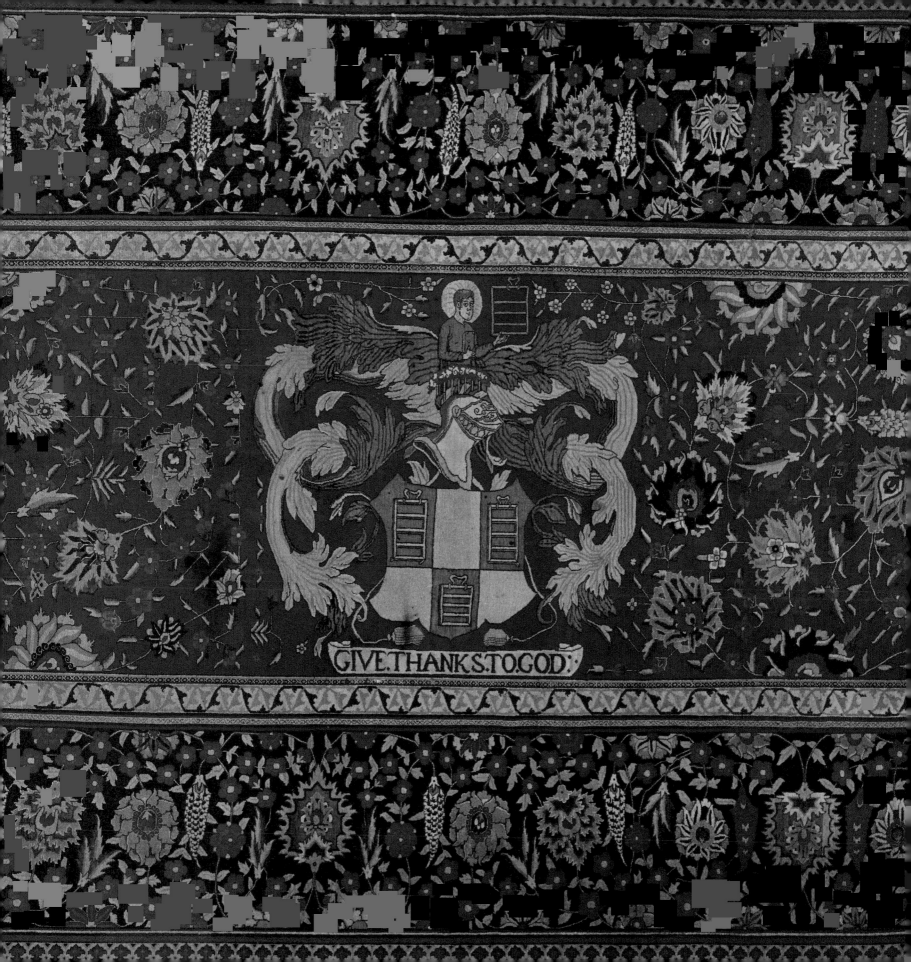

GIVE.THANKS.TO.GOD.

MUGHAL CARPET
(The Girdlers' Carpet, detail)

Date: 17th century
The Girdlers' Company, London
Dimensions: 732×229 cm (288×90 in)
Asymmetrical knot:
346,500 knots per sq. metre (224 per sq. inch)
* 63 knots per 10 cm length (16 per inch length)*
* 55 knots per 10 cm width (14 per inch width)*
Cotton warp
Cotton weft
Wool pile

One of the most splendid surviving carpets to have been woven in the seventeenth century, this rug testifies to the splendour of the reign of the Mughals, who so successfully patronized the arts and crafts and especially the craft of carpet-making, which, sponsored by them, attained the height of perfection.

This piece was made for Robert Bell (1564-1637), a prominent member of the East India Company, and presented to the Girdlers' Company in 1634, when Bell was serving as Master. The two medallions bear the arms of Robert Bell: an eagle displayed argent, in chief three fleurs-de-lys or, on an azure ground. Two other panels bear a monogram of his initials 'R.B.' in the centre of a device that is supposed to be his trade-mark.

In the centre is the company's coat-of-arms, woven in reverse. Dominating it is the figure of St Lawrence, the company's patron saint. In his hand, he holds the Gospels—perhaps the English cherished the hope of spreading the Christian faith by establishing themselves in India. In his other hand, the saint bears the instrument of his martyrdom, the grid-iron, on which he was burned alive. The grid-iron is repeated three times on the shield, and underneath runs the legend, 'Give thanks to God'.

The carpet is very long, since it was intended to cover a table. On both field and border there is a profusion of floral scrollwork with palmettes and lotus blossoms. The inner guard seems to mark the boundaries of the table top, the border being intended to hang below the table's edges.

MUGHAL CARPET
(The Fremlin Carpet)

Date: 17th century
Victoria and Albert Museum, London (I.M. 1 – 1936)
Dimensions: 579×244 cm (228×96 in)
Asymmetrical knot:
346,500 knots per sq. metre (223 per sq. inch)
* 55 knots per 10 cm length (14 per inch length)*
* 63 knots per 10 cm width (16 per inch width)*
Warp of undyed cotton
Weft of undyed cotton
Wool pile

Throughout the three and a half centuries of its history, this carpet, for which various origins have been proposed, has found its way through several continents and attracted a great many admirers. It owes its name to William Fremlin, whose arms are depicted both on the border and the field. While in the service of the East India Company between 1626 and 1644, Fremlin found himself in Ahmedabad in 1628, in Agra in 1630 and in Surat in 1633. Succeeding William Methold in 1637, Fremlin became president of the Council of the East India Company in Surat. He left India in 1644 and died in 1646.

The very elongated shape of this carpet and the wide border edging it are explained by Fremlin's intention of using it as a table cover.

Signs of Persian influence are fairly apparent in the style of the carpet, especially in the large arabesques of the border. However, the beasts disporting themselves on the field of flowers and shrubs and the birds perched on their branches are totally indigenous motifs.

In 1882 Vincent Robinson mentions this carpet in his book *Eastern Carpets*, discovering for it a Spanish origin. It was only in 1913 that *The Times* newspaper established a link between this carpet and the Fremlin family. At that time the carpet was in America. The English became interested in it, and in 1936 it was acquired by the Victoria and Albert Museum, thus returning to the country of its owner, after a lengthy odyssey.

MUGHAL TREE AND ANIMAL CARPET

Date: c. 1600
Österreichisches Museum für angewandte Kunst, Vienna
(Or. 292)
Dimensions: 235×156 cm (93×61 in)
Asymmetrical knot:
752,000 knots per sq. metre (485 per sq. inch)
*   94 knots per 10 cm length (24 per inch length)*
*   80 knots per 10 cm width (20 per inch width)*
Warp of undyed cotton
Weft of pink cotton
Pile of 2, 3 and 4 strands of wool

Among a group of carpets of symmetrical composition, it is wonderful to come upon a design that is freer in conception and brimming with life. There is, however, no lack of balance in this asymmetrical arrangement. Taking their axis from the central tree, all the elements of this pastoral scene are interrelated in total harmony.

Pairs of winged creatures perch everywhere, in the grass and flowers on the ground, in the branches of bushes and trees. This detail provides an insight into the delicate sensitivity of these people, in whose eyes the couple is both the symbol of love, which motivates all creatures, and the origin of life.

In the lower part of the design, under a tree that appears to bear rose blossoms, two confronted geese chatter to the right of the trunk, and other pairs of birds are perched on the branches to its left.

To the right of the large tree, in the centre of the pattern, a peacock spreads its tail before its partner; while on the left a cock and hen watch over their chicks. On the topmost branches cranes, returned from their distant migration, whisper lovingly to each other. Lastly, in the foliage of the upper tree, turtle-doves, hoopoes and partridges savour, in idyllic surroundings, a security unknown to man.

The colouring of the flowers and leaves and the predominantly beige plumage of the birds are highlighted perfectly by the blood-red ground—the whole carpet is a celebration of life, tenderness and elegance.

A very fitting frame is provided by the clarity and sequence of the motifs in the border: palmettes containing animal masks (probably of cats) run between two golden guard bands dotted with flowers.

MUGHAL PRAYER RUG

Date: beginning of the 17th century
Metropolitan Museum of Art, New York (Bequest of Joseph V. McMullan, 1973: 1974.149.2)
Dimensions: 155×103 cm (61×41 in)
Asymmetrical knot:
303,900/372,100 knots per sq. metre (196/240 per sq. inch)
Cotton warp
Silk weft
Wool pile

This radiant piece belongs to a special group of prayer rugs of which, unfortunately, only a few examples are known to survive.

The carpet recalls a stained-glass window of ogival form, which becomes a hymn of sheer joy when illuminated by the light of day. The motifs are simple and well-spaced, their richness deriving from the perfection of their design combined with the warmth of their colouring.

A single plant dominates the field, a chrysanthemum with fully open, golden flowers, borne on stems with foliage that varies from golden-yellow to dark blue, thus allowing the flowers to make their full brilliant impact. On the blue ground of the spandrels on either side of the apex of the ogive, edged as it were with wrought gold, sprawl more chrysanthemums, some drawn in profile.

In the principal border, on the same red ground as the field, a leafy scroll meanders elegantly, coiling around floral rosettes. Bold poppies inserted into the scroll appear at the centre of each border and at each corner. Two wide floral bands separate the border from the field of the carpet.

MUGHAL PRAYER RUG

Date: 17th century
Österreichisches Museum für angewandte Kunst, Vienna
(T 1539)
Dimensions: 155×107 cm (61×42 in)
Asymmetrical knot:
672,000 knots per sq. metre (434 per sq. inch)
  84 knots per 10 cm length (21 per inch length)
  80 knots per 10 cm width (20 per inch width)
Warp of red, green, yellow and blue silk
Weft of yellow silk
Pile of 4 strands of wool

On first impression, this is a surprising, but indubitably beautiful rug. It is clearly a prayer rug, as shown by the implied direction given to the central motif. But, as in many other carpets, this movement might equally well represent an ascent to the infinite heights of some mystery instead of the search for the divine presence in some holy place. We must allow the artist to keep his secret and simply ponder the significance of the design. Is it a sacred grove, a funerary stone, a living being, man or beast, perhaps a fish or a divinity?

Standing on a scalloped plinth of blue-black with little sprigs of red and beige flowers, this richly decorated 'grove' is profusely studded with flowers, their petals indented and quite detached from each other. A veritable feast of form and colour is the result.

Cypresses planted in pots grow on either side of this motif, their beige tones emphasizing the red ground. The upper corners of the field are adorned with a graceful and refined pattern in which delicate branches of flowers and rhomboids are interlaced upon a gold ground. The border is edged by two light guard bands of equal width and formed by a succession of small flower clusters that seem to dance a farandole against the green ground around the larger species set at regular intervals.

MUGHAL TREE AND ANIMAL CARPET
(Lahore)

Date: beginning of the 17th century (period of Jahangir)
Metropolitan Museum of Art, New York (Gift of J. Pierpont Morgan, 1917: 17.190.858)
Dimensions: 833×289 cm (328×114 in)
Asymmetrical knot:
176,000 knots per sq. metre (114 per sq. inch)
  44 knots per 10 cm length (11 per inch length)
  40 knots per 10 cm width (10 per inch width)
Warp of undyed cotton
Weft of pink cotton
Wool pile

In this carpet from the Mughal period, the scene sparkles with exuberance thanks to the Mughals' predilection for their much-loved red.

One is struck straightaway by an unusual feature of the pattern, which is repeated four times with each section just above the next one, but reversed from left to right: the right-hand motifs in one repeat are on the left in the next.

The carpet depicts a scene from nature: a forest planted with palms and flowering trees inhabited by a multitude of birds, subject to the law of the jungle, represented by tigers and lions hunting ibexes—in the lower corner of the design, a lion has an ibex locked between its jaws.

Once again a constant search for diversity is evident. For although the designs are repeated and the motifs, drawn in similar fashion, match one another, the colours are reversed to create a sense of mystery where simple repetition was expected.

Between two identical narrow bands, the border is ornamented with geometric forms. Rectangular medallions terminating in hexagonal stars and studded with roses are interspersed regularly with star-shaped hexagonal medallions set with a single rose.

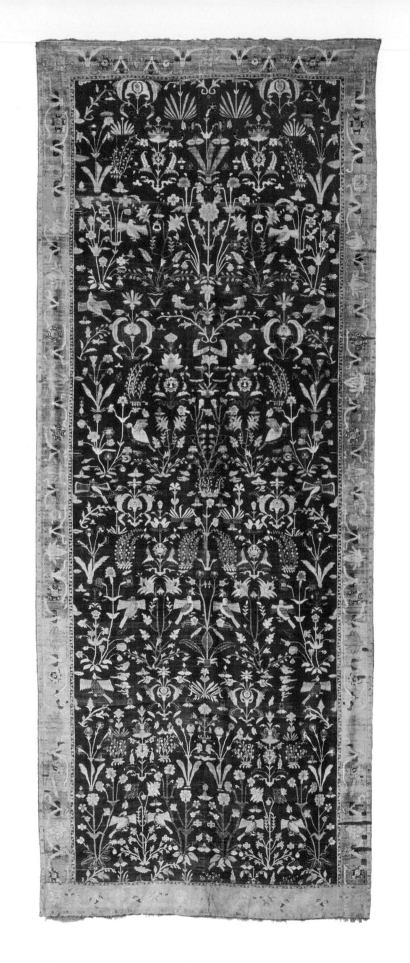

MUGHAL CARPET

Date: 17th century
Musée historique des Tissus, Lyons (24 620)
Dimensions: 340×135 cm (134×53 in)
Asymmetrical knot:
1,440,000 knots per sq. metre (929 per sq. inch)
*   120 knots per 10 cm length (30 per inch length)*
*   120 knots per 10 cm width (30 per inch width)*
Warp of 2 strands of yellow silk
Weft of pink silk
Silk pile

By its dimensions a runner, this carpet has the appearance of a path strewn with flower-beds and shrubs, where a flock of birds with outstretched wings disport themselves.

The composition is symmetrical in parts, since the motifs that are on the same level horizontally correspond exactly in shape and position, while this is not the case in the vertical plane. The result gives an impression of escaping into an enchanted world, far from the beaten track, where flowers grow and birds fly where they please.

The arabesques in the soft green border are encrusted with roses and other flowers that alternate the colours of the field: yellow-gold, red and blue. The gentle tones of the border allow the central area to achieve its full impact.

MUGHAL CARPET (detail)

Date: 1625
Maharaja Sawai Man Singh II Museum, City Palace, Jaipur
Dimensions: 1750×492 cm (689×194 in)
Asymmetrical knot:
87,500 knots per sq. metre (56 per sq. inch)
  25 knots per 10 cm length (6 per inch length)
  35 knots per 10 cm width (9 per inch width)
Warp of 3 strands of undyed cotton
Weft of 2 strands of undyed cotton
Wool pile

Only a great prince would be in a position to acquire and display in a suitable setting such an enormous piece, with a surface area of 86 m² (109 yd²). According to the records of the City Palace Museum in Jaipur, the carpet was woven in Herat in 1625 for Maharaja Raya Singh I of Amber.

In the sixteenth and seventeenth centuries, Herat formed part of the Mughal empire. Emperor Akbar had established a carpet manufactory there, but the fact that Herat later became a Persian town sometimes creates confusion: carpets made in Herat during the Mughal period are sometimes incorrectly assumed to have been woven in Persia. However, their palette and certain elements of the motifs do not deceive, for they are clearly of the Mughal period when the art of the Indian carpet attained the peak of perfection.

The movement expressed in this piece is of consummate grace and is created by the curved leaves that rise, poised like golden sheaves, in the centre of the field, while others in darker tones spread all over. The movement is further underlined by the light-coloured tendrils that link the motifs without forming a tangled network. This carpet is a model of clarity, elegance and exuberance; the multiplicity of forms, flowers and palmettes intermarry without overwhelming one another.

Large palmettes, decorated with gold, red and blue, and separated by a quintuple arrangement of flowers, appear on the blue-black border. The outer guard stripe is double; the inner one shows traces of greenery amid small red and blue flowers set in pairs. Perfection on such a grand scale demonstrates matchless taste and skill.

MUGHAL CARPET (detail)

Date: beginning of the 17th century
Maharaja Sawai Man Singh II Museum, City Palace, Jaipur
Dimensions: 716×300 cm (282×118 in)
Asymmetrical knot:
157,500 knots per sq. metre (102 per sq. inch)
   45 knots per 10 cm length (11 per inch length)
   35 knots per 10 cm width (9 per inch width)
Warp of 3 strands of undyed cotton
Weft of 3 strands of undyed cotton
Wool pile

The palmettes on the blue-black border, encircled by foliage like those on the field, have the dimensions of palmettes on Indian rugs, but they seem rounder and less spiky in treatment. The two narrow bands enclosing the border are spattered with enchanting tiny flowers absolutely faithful to tradition.

Carpets of this type are often called Indo-Isfahan, which denotes their dual origin. Although the design is Persian, this carpet was made in India. This example, for instance, must have been made in the workshops at Herat.

It must be remembered that the Mughal rulers, desirous of promoting the carpet industry, enlisted the best available craftsmen, from Persia in particular. Accustomed to the classic motifs of their homeland, Persian weavers continued to use them when they settled in India, adapting the motifs to the style and palette of the country. This is particularly apparent in the border motifs, where the whole effect encapsulates the genius of the Mughal period.

The red field conveys a dazzling exuberance and is resplendent with blue and gold palmettes, back to back, flanked by perfectly denticulated large green leaves, lilies, daisies, lotus blossoms and other flowers of so many varieties and colours that one cannot begin to name them.

MUGHAL CARPET (detail)

Date: beginning of the 17th century
Maharaja Sawai Man Singh II Museum, City Palace, Jaipur
Dimensions: 1158×442 cm (456×174 in)
Asymmetrical knot:
200,000 knots per sq. metre (129 per sq. inch)
 40 knots per 10 cm length (10 per inch length)
 50 knots per 10 cm width (13 per inch width)
Warp of 4 strands of undyed cotton
Weft of 2 strands of undyed cotton
Wool pile

symbolizing, at least to begin with, the life-sustaining moisture of the heavens.

The structure of a carpet, together with the design of the motifs and colour variations, allows us to determine with some precision the date and place of its manufacture. In fact, there are some subjects—flowers, birds and mythological, human or animal scenes—that belong to a particular country. Imported subjects were only used after being subjected to easily recognizable modifications. And the colours derived from natural dyes according to local practice are clearly distinguishable from those of other origins. Thus, the *boteh-miri* is a typical Kashmiri flower, and the Mughal shade of red an inimitable Indian dye. The palmettes imported from Iran are drawn on a larger scale in India and treated in a manner different from that used in their country of origin.

In the carpet opposite we see the clear red and large palmettes of the time. But there is also a device inspired by the Chinese *chi*, a wavy band called the 'cloudband'. This is a common feature on oriental knotted carpets,

MUGHAL CARPET (detail)

Date: *beginning of the 17th century*
Maharaja Sawai Man Singh II Museum, City Palace, Jaipur
Dimensions: *937×292 cm (369×115 in)*
Asymmetrical knot:
140,000 knots per sq. metre (90 per sq. inch)
  40 knots per 10 cm length (10 per inch length)
  35 knots per 10 cm width (9 per inch width)
Warp of 4 strands of undyed cotton
Weft of 3 strands of undyed cotton
Wool pile

This carpet must have been woven on commission for a particular location, for it could not be accommodated in an ordinary room due to its unusual dimensions: over 9 metres (29 ft 6 in) in length and just under 3 metres (9 ft 10 in) in width.

The field with its multiplicity of detached motifs is of incomparable richness. The motifs that do correspond in form and position differ frequently in the distribution of their colours. In addition to the popular palmettes, other stylized flowers stand out, possibly begonias, which exist in great variety in India. Leafy fronds of blossom twine exuberantly and freely around the motifs on the red ground. There is a wide range of colours, from dark to pale blue, from ochre to beige or ivory, from red to rose-pink.

The border demonstrates a certain affinity with that of the preceding carpet. It consists of large palmettes, arranged reciprocally and delicately drawn, interspersed with a quintuple floral arrangement. The remarkable skill of the designer is evident in the colour layout of each motif.

The narrow guard stripes run between gold bands. The ground of the outer one is like a red ribbon adorned with a garland of beige flowers with gold centres. The double inner guard band contains two stripes: one band golden with a sequence of small Y-shaped motifs of the same blue as the border's ground, the other band a lighter blue, bearing delightful small flowers interlinked by their stems.

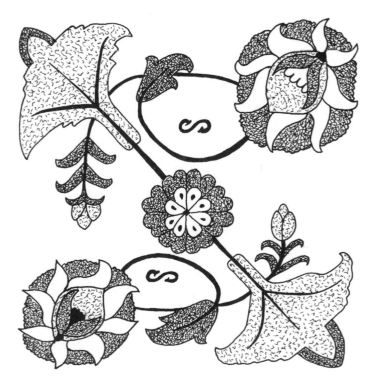

MUGHAL CARPET (detail)

Date: beginning of the 17th century
Maharaja Sawai Man Singh II Museum, City Palace, Jaipur
Dimensions: 937×292 cm (369×115 in)
Asymmetrical knot:
180,000 knots per sq. metre (116 per sq. inch)
40 knots per 10 cm length (10 per inch length)
45 knots per 10 cm width (11 per inch width)
Warp of 3 strands of undyed cotton
Weft of 3 strands of undyed cotton
Wool pile

This carpet is one of a group that has aroused much controversy among experts, both with regard to their place of manufacture and the influences that inspired them. This particular carpet has been given diverse designations: Indo-Isfahan, Herat, Shah Abbas, Isfahan, Hispano-Moresque, Indo-Persian. The most likely explanation is that this carpet was woven in Herat, where it was bought by the Maharaja of Amber, Raya Singh I, when Herat was part of the Mughal empire.

The dimensions and colouring of the palmettes differ from those found on Persian rugs. Here magnificent gold or dark blue palmettes are caught in a network of small flowers and foliage that drifts all over the red field. The palmettes are grouped in pairs, either confronted or back to back. The elongated bi-coloured leaves flanking them provide the pattern with movement, their golden centres most frequently outlined by light or dark blue.

The large reciprocal palmettes on the blue-black ground of the border are enclosed by similar lanceolate leaves, but in a richer palette, in which red and blue predominate. The ground of the guard bands is red on the outside and ochre inside; they are embellished with a sequence of little flowers resembling tiny points of light.

MUGHAL CARPET (detail)

Date: beginning of the 17th century
Maharaja Sawai Man Singh II Museum, City Palace, Jaipur
Dimensions: 1115×434 cm (439×171 in)
Asymmetrical knot:
225,000 knots per sq. metre (145 per sq. inch)
 50 knots per 10 cm length (13 per inch length)
 45 knots per 10 cm width (11 per inch width)
Warp of 4 strands of undyed cotton
Weft of 2 strands of undyed cotton
Wool pile

The size of this medallion is the most striking feature of
this very large carpet, of which a detail is reproduced
opposite. Almost elliptical in form, the motif is
undoubtedly handsome. Four golden palmettes and a
whole array of small red, beige and gold flowers on a dark
blue ground burst from the lively red centre, scattered
with little flowers towards the delicately wrought edges.
In relation to the surrounding motifs, the size of the motif
shown in detail is unusual (37 cm [14.6 in]); it is
two-thirds greater than is usual for traditional motifs in a
carpet of comparable size.

   The same is true for the border palmettes, equally
splendid and with subtle colour combinations; they
assume a position of importance amidst the network of
smaller, very jagged motifs worked in an especially rich
palette.

The border is contained within two guard stripes; visible
here is the beige one beaded with tiny flowers.

MUGHAL CARPET (detail)

Date: mid-17th century
Maharaja Sawai Man Singh II Museum, City Palace, Jaipur
Dimensions: 848×457 cm (334×180 in)
Asymmetrical knot:
112,000 knots per sq. metre (72 per sq. inch)
   32 knots per 10 cm length (8 per inch length)
   35 knots per 10 cm width (9 per inch width)
Warp of 2 strands of four-ply undyed cotton
Weft of 3 strands of undyed cotton
Wool pile

This carpet is unfortunately heavily worn, making it difficult to read, especially with regard to the colours. The red field, its brilliance still visible despite being worn, is covered with medallions forming a blue lattice of sorts, broad and intricate. There are two kinds of medallions: some rather oval in shape, others cruciform and pinched at top and bottom. Each medallion encloses a pyramidal bouquet of six identical flowers with buds and foliage below. Some of these flowers are completely stylized; those with blue centres edged with gold are probably begonias, a very popular plant in India; the perfectly sculpted variety with a red corolla ringed with gold are undoubtedly roses.

The main border bears rosettes paired with twin leaves having gold veins; these are separated by two red and blue palmettes, back to back.

Six narrow bands, three on either side, contain the border. The widest of these are strewn with two varieties of flower: roses and a campanula-like bell on a light ground. Dark motifs separate the flowers so that their brilliance has its full impact.

MUGHAL CARPET

Date: mid-17th century
Maharaja Sawai Man Singh II Museum, City Palace, Jaipur
Dimensions: 425×272/171 cm (167×107/67 in)
Asymmetrical knot:
250,000 knots per sq. metre (161 per sq. inch)
*   50 knots per 10 cm length (13 per inch length)*
*   50 knots per 10 cm width (13 per inch width)*
Warp of 4 strands of undyed cotton
Weft of beige and red cotton
Wool pile

Mr Yaduendra Sahai of the City Palace Museum in Jaipur has conducted research into the way in which both this carpet and the following one, also of unusual shape, were originally used. Failing to discover, in the palace at Amber, the residence of the Maharaja Mirza Raja Jai Singh I, any correspondence relating to these carpets purchased in 1656, he puts forward the theory that since the Maharaja possessed some ten or so of these pieces at the time, they must have been used to furnish the tents erected for hunting parties. Since hunting was the favourite pastime of the ruler, this supposition is perfectly feasible. Even today, in the Middle East, families spreading out very handsome rugs in their tents are a familiar sight.

The arrangement of the motifs makes it clear that this carpet was woven for a predetermined purpose. On a brilliant red ground are bouquets, not in vases or urns, but in clumps of three to five specimens, the uneven number permitting a balanced arrangement in pyramidal or fan shape. There are an astonishing variety of species and colours. The variously shaped corollas are of red, pink, ochre and beige, all with centres of different colours. The foliage is also rendered more lively by the remarkable colour contrasts.

The dark blue border running between two golden fillets is studded with red-centred ochre flowers set in their own leafy foliage with other small flower buds.

MUGHAL CARPET

Date: mid-17th century
Maharaja Sawai Man Singh II Museum, City Palace, Jaipur
Dimensions: 416×275/160 cm (164×108/63 in)
Asymmetrical knot:
360,000 knots per sq. metre (232 per sq. inch)
  60 knots per 10 cm length (15 per inch length)
  60 knots per 10 cm width (15 per inch width)
Warp of 5 strands of undyed cotton
Weft of 2 strands of two-ply red and beige cotton
Wool pile

This carpet, like the previous example, must have been
used to decorate the Maharaja's tent. It displays two
curious features. Firstly, its shape was dictated by that of
the tent, totally different from a room in an ordinary
house. Secondly, the pile appears in partial relief. In the
beige flowers interlinked by red stems on the dark blue
border, the petals of the corollas are formed by the warp
and weft only, without any pile, while the red centres are
knotted, throwing them into relief. Similarly, on the
narrow guards, small brown details are knotted, while the
remainder is left without pile, thus adding to its firmness.
This is a curious and somewhat rare technique. According
to the attached label, the carpet was purchased in Lahore
in 1656 by the Maharaja Mirza Raja Jai Singh I.

The motifs of the field are to a great extent similar to
those of the preceding carpet, with clusters of richly
coloured flowers of varied composition. But here the
flowers are disposed in a more loosely spaced arrangement.

MUGHAL CARPET (detail)

Date: 17th century
Maharaja Sawai Man Singh II Museum, City Palace, Jaipur
Dimensions: 300×124 cm (118×49 in)
Asymmetrical knot:
810,000 knots per sq. metre (522 per sq. inch)
  90 knots per 10 cm length (23 per inch length)
  90 knots per 10 cm width (23 per inch width)
Warp of 4 strands of red and white silk
Weft of 3 strands of red silk
Wool pile

This carpet, featuring the loveliest of reds and extremely fine in structure, is unfortunately in very poor condition. According to Dr Asok Kumar Das, director of the museum, the golden-yellow flowers are *champas*, offered only to deities and monarchs. They are drawn and knotted by the hand of a master, as are the roses and carnations merging with them that bathe the field with elegance and light.

In the twin confronted medallions is a species resembling the Princess Charlotte passion-flower, a very common plant throughout India. In the opinion of the botanist L.H. Bailey, the name of the genus *Passiflora* derives from a legend telling of Spanish and Italian travellers journeying through India, who discovered in these flowers a reminder of the Crucifixion of Christ. The ten petals represent the ten Apostles at the foot of the Cross (Peter and Judas having been absent), and the little corona in the centre of the corolla the Crown of Thorns. The five stamens symbolize the five wounds or the five nails. The three-part pistil represents the lash that scourged Christ, and the leaves the hands of His tormentors.

The border pattern on its red ground is very similar to that of the field in the style of the flowers, although the stems interlinking them are golden, while on the field they are green. The guards are especially pretty, with their small flowers of dark blue, yellow and red winding around on a light ground.

MUGHAL CARPET (detail)

Date: mid-17th century
Maharaja Sawai Man Singh II Museum, City Palace, Jaipur
Dimensions: 900×284 cm (354×111 in)
Asymmetrical knot:
140,000 knots per sq. metre (90 per sq. inch)
   40 knots per 10 cm length (10 per inch length)
   35 knots per 10 cm width (9 per inch width)
Warp of 3 strands of undyed cotton
Weft of 2 strands of three-ply pink cotton
Wool pile

The dimensions of this very long and relatively narrow carpet indicate that it was the object of a special commission intended for a predetermined location. In fact this is confirmed by a label on the reverse of the carpet. It was purchased by the Maharaja Mirza Raja Jai Singh I of Amber, apparently for a room in one of his official residences.

This carpet is thus of later manufacture than others preserved in the museum of Jaipur that date from the beginning of the seventeenth century. This is not noticeable, however, either in the design of the field with its palmettes, large flowers and scrolls, or in the incomparable colouring, which are still of the classic Mughal period. However, the border differs clearly from classic Mughal rugs. It is formed of small medallions, each bearing a flower and skilfully interlinked on three levels. The colours flow with rare profusion from dark blue to light beige, passing through most of the usual palette.

Two guard stripes frame the border; the inner one is the most original and patterned with a garland of stylized motifs not found on earlier rugs.

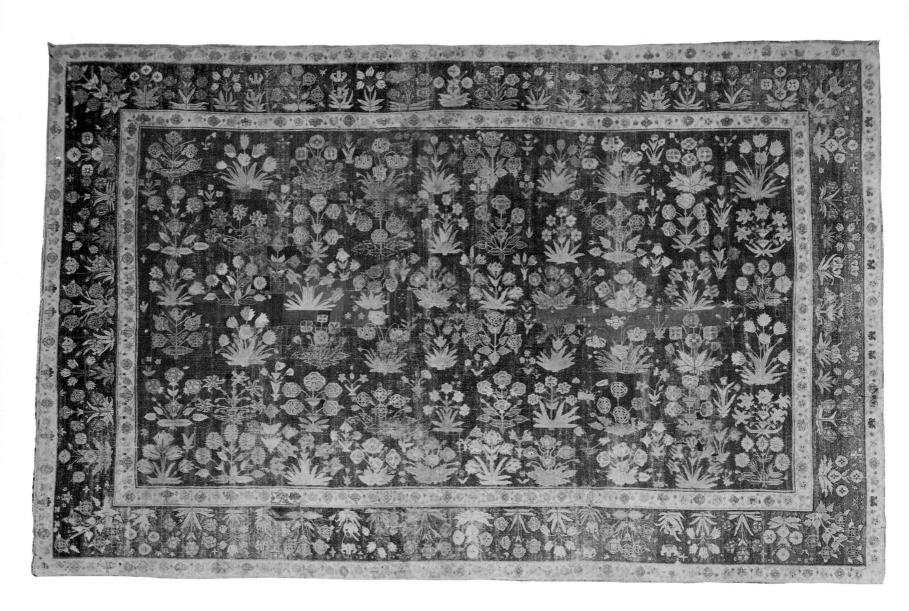

MUGHAL CARPET

Date: 17th century
Keir Collection, London
Dimensions: 309×467 cm (122×184 in)
Asymmetrical knot:
380,000 knots per sq. metre (245 per sq. inch)
* 69 knots per 10 cm length (18 per inch length)*
* 55 knots per 10 cm width (14 per inch width)*
Warp of undyed cotton
Weft of undyed cotton
Wool pile

This is a typically Indian carpet, made in the reign of the Mughals to decorate the vast rooms of the palace at Amber. It is quite apparent, on examination, that the Maharaja's wish was to spread on the marble floors of his sumptuous palace carpets strewn with flowers, not merely those of the most decorative variety, but also those with symbolic connotations of nobility: rose, lotus, tulip, carnation, lily and iris. These flowers are arranged all over, both on the field and the border, in small clumps amid foliage.

This carpet is unusual in that its width is greater than its length. According to A.F. Kendrick, this was unique to the carpets woven for the palace at Amber and incorporated into the collection of the palace at Jaipur in 1875.

The brilliant effect of the gold motifs on the red ground of the field is solidly offset by the dark blue frame of the border, surrounded by two golden guard bands.

FRAGMENT OF A MUGHAL CARPET

Date: 17th century
Türk ve Islam Eserleri Müzesi, Istanbul (TIEM 105)
Dimensions: 430×270 cm (169×106 in)
Asymmetrical knot:
220,900 knots per sq. metre (142 per sq. inch)
*   47 knots per 10 cm length (12 per inch length)*
*   47 knots per 10 cm width (12 per inch width)*
Warp of 6 strands of undyed cotton
Weft of 3 strands of undyed and red cotton
Wool pile

On this family prayer rug, or *saf*, with signs of Persian influence, four colours predominate: Mughal red, dark blue, green and ivory. They are used in contrast here, to emphasize each other.

The rounded outlines of the *mihrabs* on the field add to the impression of gentleness in the design; the upper part of each arch is bordered by a small red band serving as a background for golden threads. Each *mihrab* has a delicately worked central medallion in a colour that contrasts with its field and around which pretty roses form a chain. Two arabesques extend the medallion above and below, seeming to anchor it in place.

The spandrels—blue or green when the field is red, red when the field is blue or green—have an ivory-coloured decor of random leaves and flowers in excellent taste.

On the red ground of the border, reminiscent of Persian carpets, are dark blue, meandering cloudbands winding among the ivory tendrils on which leaves and red-centred flowers grow.

The two guard bands are golden ribbons: the inner one is encrusted with tiny, equally spaced, ivory flowers; the outer one, which resembles embroidery more than weaving, is adorned with beautiful red roses. The large roses grow amidst bunches of green leaves joined together by small roses, like children holding hands and dancing in a round.

A PAIR OF MUGHAL PRAYER RUGS

Date: late 17th or early 18th century
Keir Collection, London
Dimensions: 242×131 cm (95×52 in); 260×131 cm (102×52 in)
Asymmetrical knot:
157,500 knots per sq. metre (102 per sq. inch)
  45 knots per 10 cm length (11 per inch length)
  35 knots per 10 cm width (9 per inch width)
Warp of undyed cotton
Weft of undyed cotton
Wool pile

A prayer rug is usually conceived to accommodate a single person, the encounter with God being an intimate and personal act. The typical prayer rug includes on the field a *mihrab*, or prayer arch, a motif that indicates where the believer must kneel to carry out his devotions. In these examples, one believer can kneel in each of the three arches, so that they can rightly be called 'family prayer rugs'.

The two pieces are influenced by the architecture of the period. Three arches are supported by columns with basin-shaped capitals that seem to be awaiting floral decoration. At the foot of each column, a little plant flowers, giving rise to an arabesque.

Trees occupy the arcades. The central one bears pomegranates; the ravishing flowers on the other two are reversed in colours.

The colours are typically Indian, but the border—a gold path inscribed with a sequence of leafy fronds and flowers, light and free—is of Persian inspiration.

MUGHAL PRAYER RUG

Date: *beginning of the 17th century*
(period of Jahangir)
Thyssen-Bornemisza Collection, Castagnola
Dimensions: 124×90 cm (49×35 in)
Asymmetrical knot:
686,400 knots per sq. metre (443 per sq. inch)
  78 knots per 10 cm length (20 per inch length)
  88 knots per 10 cm width (22 per inch width)
Warp of white, beige, gold, yellow and blue silk
Weft of red silk
Wool pile

This prayer rug is known as the Aynard Rug after a previous owner. It is so lustrous that it was long considered to be made of silk, but there is no silk in the pile, and its exceptional delicacy derives from the very fine wool of Kashmir, used in former days for the manufacture of shawls. On the basis of design and quality, it can be dated within the reign of the Emperor Jahangir (1605-27), who encouraged artists to choose their subjects from the finest offerings of nature, especially birds and flowers.

The lateral borders indicate that the carpet has been cut from a larger piece. It may have originally formed part of a multiple prayer rug, composed of several parts, each identical to this one.

The flowers of the majestic plant growing within the *mihrab* and unfurling over the warm red field are of the genus *Passiflora*, which grow so prolifically in India. The upper corners of the field are almost like sheer veils through which the red ground of the field can be spied; they are scattered with exquisite five- or six-petalled pink flowers.

On the longitudinal borders are small clusters of carnations on a beige ground, while the narrow guard stripes bear a sequence of small flowers similar to those in the upper corners of the field.

MUGHAL CARPET

Date: 17th century
Thyssen-Bornemisza Collection, Castagnola
Dimensions: 473×209 cm (186×82 in)
Asymmetrical knot:
84,000 knots per sq. metre (54 per sq. inch)
  28 knots per 10 cm length (7 per inch length)
  30 knots per 10 cm width (8 per inch width)
Cotton warp
Cotton weft
Wool pile

This piece, known in the Thyssen-Bornemisza Collection as the Benguiat Carpet, is of the same style and palette as the example inventoried as No. 1 in the Jaipur museum and reproduced here on page 86.

On a red ground, among a great number of scrolls, are saffron-yellow and dark blue palmettes, denticulated with great artistry. Leafy foliage with blossoms provides an interlinking tracery that embellishes the field with its varied forms and harmonious lines.

The dark blue border is of the same pattern as the Jaipur piece: large palmettes, some ochre with red and blue centres, others blue with ochre centres. Each is framed by five palmettes of smaller scale, also of blue and ochre.

Two guard bands frame the border: one is very narrow, the other wider. Both are dotted with a pattern of charming, equally spaced blue flowers interlinked by stems with buds and foliage.

FRAGMENT OF A MUGHAL CARPET

Date: end of the 17th century
Thyssen-Bornemisza Collection, Castagnola
Dimensions: 160×106 cm (63×42 in)
Asymmetrical knot:
84,100 knots per sq. metre (54 per sq. inch)
   29 knots per 10 cm length (7 per inch length)
   29 knots per 10 cm width (7 per inch width)
Warp of undyed cotton
Weft of grey cotton
Wool pile

The pattern of the example seen on the fragment opposite presents similarities with the Benguiat Carpet in the same collection illustrated on page 116. It follows logically that this carpet also came from Herat, where a manufactory was established by the Mughal Emperor Akbar.

The large palmettes on the field, in yellow-ochre or dark blue, are delicately drawn and encircled by wavy garlands of light blue ribbons of the *chi* type. The field is lined with elegantly curving branches, bearing flowers and foliage of contrasting colours, which render them more obvious.

The dark blue ground of the border is decorated with palmettes arranged more closely than on the Benguiat Carpet and more varied in detail than in colouring. They are separated by a smaller palmette encircled by its own stem.

On the two guard bands—one on a light beige ground, and the other with the same red ground as the field—runs a pattern of similar small flowers; the colouring of the petals and foliage vary alternately.

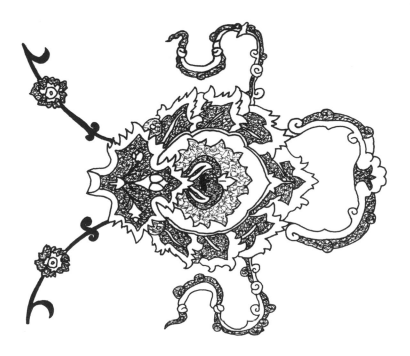

FRAGMENT OF A MUGHAL CARPET

Date: 17th century
Keir Collection, London
Dimensions: 94×79 cm (37×31 in)
Asymmetrical knot:
813,400 knots per sq. metre (525 per sq. inch)
98 knots per 10 cm length (25 per inch length)
83 knots per 10 cm width (21 per inch width)
Warp of undyed cotton
Silk weft
Wool pile

From the outset one obtains the clear impression that this carpet is only a fragment of a larger piece. First of all, the border is too scanty, and one feels that the weaver was content just to fix the strands at the sides. Furthermore, the motifs have been cut off too abruptly at the sides, whereas in the middle each motif forms a perfect ensemble. Lastly, the size of the motifs is out of proportion with the surface on which they are contained.

The knotting of this carpet is extremely fine. The ensemble to which it belonged must have been of rare beauty and of inestimable value.

On a ground of the so alluring Mughal red, bouquets of roses, carnations, lotus flowers, irises and lilies have the appearance of being arranged in a wonderfully wrought lattice that characterizes the entire composition. The dark colours—especially the greens—emphasize, support and sustain the light tones.

In some prayer rugs of this period, identical flowers are encountered, presented in the same style.

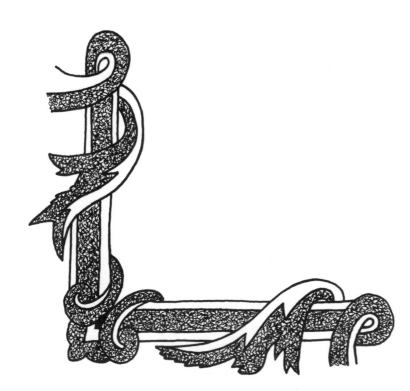

MUGHAL TREE CARPET

Date: early 17th century (Shah Jahan period)
Frick Collection, New York
Dimensions: 227×192 cm (89.5×75.5 in)
Asymmetrical knot:
891,500 knots per sq. metre (575 per sq. inch)
*   100 knots per 10 cm length (25 per inch length)*
*   92 knots per 10 cm width (23 per inch width)*
Cotton warp
Cotton weft
Wool pile

An impression of gentleness is conveyed in this carpet by the particularly delicate palette of greens and pinks arrayed over the claret-red ground.

The design appears simple, but is rare indeed. Three rows of trees, forming a succession of terraces separated by garlands of flowers, are hardly the result of careful search for originality, which is why one is tempted to look for some religious significance in the composition. Perhaps it expresses the stages of ascent from the cypresses on the bottom to the knowledge of a trine divinity, in which the central element has precedence over the other two. Such an interpretation seems all the more fitting since this carpet comes from the shrine of the holy city of Ardebil in Iran, to which it found its way either as a gift or as the spoils of war.

The flowers adorning the trees and the lotus blossoms and tulips that brighten the flower-beds relieve the somewhat heavy motifs and create true enchantment.

The large scrolls in the border that float on a blood-coloured ground amidst tulips and lotus are distinguished by their purity of design and majestic aspect. The two soft green guards, also elegantly flowered, frame the border without in any way detracting from its impact.

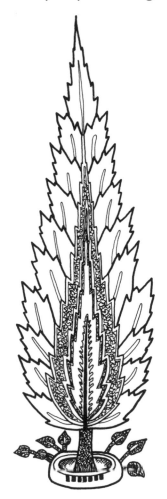

MUGHAL CARPET (detail)
(Lahore)

Date: beginning of the 17th century (period of Jahangir)
Metropolitan Museum of Art, New York (Gift of J. Pierpont Morgan, 1917: 17.190.857)
Dimensions: 923×338 cm (363×133 in)
Asymmetrical knot:
210,000 knots per sq. metre (135 per sq. inch)
   52 knots per 10 cm length (13 per inch length)
   40 knots per 10 cm width (10 per inch width)
Warp of undyed cotton
Weft of pink cotton
Wool pile

Only a detail of this splendid carpet is shown here, because of its enormous size. If reduced, some of the details would no longer have been perceptible, while they are quite clear when shown in this manner.

Carpets had to cover a very large area (this one has an area of no less than 31 m^2 [37 yd^2]) in order to fulfil their role of adorning the large state rooms of palaces, audience chambers, etc. A particular requirement in state rooms was that the carpet be lively in colouring. This is the reason for the ubiquitous use of the strong Mughal red on the field and borders of this masterly carpet—to attract attention.

The motifs within the pattern are large and clear. In beige or golden-yellow they sparkle on the red ground. The basic motifs are palmettes of similar size, distinguished by differences in formation and colour. They are aligned vertically or horizontally, two by two, face to face or back to back. Spikes of flowers and foliage enclose them subtly, emphasizing the brilliance of each palmette.

Of the three borders, the widest one is decorated with a chain of cartouches and medallions containing an appealing arrangement of flowers, palmettes and arabesques. Around the panels and medallions meander 'cloudbands', a familiar theme on carpets throughout the East.

The four bands containing the borders are paired with similar motifs, but reversed in colour. On the inner one, flowers are set within small hexagons, while on the outer one the flowers spring from a curling tendril.

Even after long scrutiny, a carpet such as this reveals new details that are a constant source of wonderment.

MUGHAL FLORAL CARPET

Date: mid-17th century (period of Shah Jahan)
Metropolitan Museum of Art, New York (Bequest of Florence
Waterbury and Rogers Fund, 1970: 1970.321)
Dimensions: 426×200 cm (168×79 in)
Asymmetrical knot:
242,000 knots per sq. metre (156 per sq. inch)
Cotton warp
Cotton weft
Wool pile

Despite the lovely, well-preserved red, identical in field and border, and the seven superposed rows of flowers covering the surface, there is no trace of monotony in this carpet. The flower sprays are varied in species and size and include, among others, carnations, roses, lilies, irises and tulips. If the same type of flower recurs in the same row, its position is altered: for example, in one lilies are shown between tulips, then tulips between lilies. Although the decorative elements are repeated time and again, they are arranged for variety and form a harmonious ensemble. The border bears smaller motifs of palmettes and rosettes planted among blossoming foliage and forms a perfect frame for the field, even though border and field are of the same colour. Two golden guard bands run alongside the border.

Finally, the light tones of the basic elements (beige, yellow, golden-yellow and pink), emphasized occasionally by dark shades of blue and green, form tiny pools of light that serve to bring the carpet to life.

MUGHAL CARPET

Date: 17th century
Institute of Arts, Detroit (Gift of Mr and Mrs Edsel B Ford: 29 242)
Dimensions: 366×178 cm (144×70 in)
Asymmetrical knot:
360,000 knots per sq. metre (232 per sq. inch)
Cotton warp
Cotton weft
Wool pile

This is an unusual pattern. A great many examples of carpets from the Mughal period bear medallions, generally with an imposing and highly elaborate central device containing a succession of motifs of fairly similar contours. The colouring of the motifs differs, however, and the small floral motif occupying the centre usually has the appearance of a jewel set in fine metalwork.

This carpet has two medallions of stylized palmettes. Although they possess none of the usual rich elements, they are no less handsome in their simplicity. The colours are very subtly positioned to give depth to the carpet and are in perfect harmony with the rest of the field, with its palmettes skirting the lateral borders and spandrels formed of fragments of the actual medallions. Elongated lanceolate leaves—pointing either outwards or towards the centre—frame clusters of flowers whose horizontal position provides a sort of consolidating framework for the whole carpet. The branches linking the flowers and palmettes are also well-organized to embellish and enliven the field.

The border bears an undulating pattern of arabesques interspersed with palmettes; it creates a feeling of powerful movement between the festoons of the narrow guard bands escorting it.

MUGHAL CARPET

Date: 17th century
Collection of the Museum of the Shrine, Mashhad
Dimensions: 464×283 cm (183×111 in)
Asymmetrical knot:
920,000 knots per sq. metre (593 per sq. inch)
*   92 knots per 10 cm length (23 per inch length)*
*   100 knots per 10 cm width (25 per inch width)*
Warp of silk of various colours
Weft of red silk
Wool pile

The description 'Mughal' has been applied to the classic period of the Indian carpet. Though they created their empire in the sixteenth century by force of arms and brought about the unification of India, these warriors did not lack nobility. They gave great impetus to literature and the arts, especially to the art of carpet-making which attained the heights of perfection under their reign. Carpets were a prominent feature of the magnificent palaces the Mughals constructed.

Although this carpet unfortunately shows signs of a tear and the subsequent repair is not one of the most successful, the carpet is still strikingly beautiful. Within the delicately worked lattice of gold thread forming lozenges is either a carnation, a rose or a palmette. Each of these large flowers is ringed by a variety of small yellow, pink and red ones, like a planet by its satellites. Everything on this bright red ground sparkles like stars.

The border consists of a 'necklace' of floral medallions scattered on a blue ground, enclosed by two guard bands. The inner one—resembling a gold ribbon ornamented by carnations—is reminiscent of the work of a master-jeweller.

MUGHAL CARPET

Date: 17th century
Collection of the Museum of the Shrine, Mashhad
Dimensions: 550×400 cm (217×157 in)
Asymmetrical knot:
920,000 knots per sq. metre (593 per sq. inch)
*   92 knots per 10 cm length (23 per inch length)*
*   100 knots per 10 cm width (25 per inch width)*
Warp of silk of various colours
Weft of red silk
Wool pile

The border lacks its usual enclosure of a small guard band to separate it from the field; none the less, the demarcation is clear, since the grille on the field stops at the border, which is composed of a row of flowers of varying dimensions, rich in form, and coloured in a gentle and luminous combination of beige and pink.

This example is typical of the Mughal dynasty during the seventeenth century, as is shown by the fineness of the knotting and the generosity of scale, by the patterns and the colouring, particularly the Mughal red ground colour.

This carpet is covered with an overall grille of gold lines with lozenge-shaped openings. Since such golden lattices appear so frequently as a motif on carpets of this provenance, they must have been in evidence as architectural features in the palaces of Agra and Jaipur, usually opening onto magnificent flower gardens, but perhaps onto state rooms too, and onto drawing rooms and boudoirs.

In each compartment is a single large flower—a rose, a carnation or a lily—accompanied here and there by smaller ones. These are interlinked by tendrils with unobtrusive foliage that leads from one to the other without respect for the boundaries defined by the outline of the grille.

FRAGMENT OF A MUGHAL CARPET

Date: late 16th or early 17th century
Kunstmuseum, Düsseldorf (13548)
Dimensions: 71.5×56.5 cm (28×22 in)
Asymmetrical knot:
960,000 knots per sq. metre (619 per sq. inch)
Silk warp
Silk weft
Silk pile

The design of this carpet fragment is identical with that in the London example (see the following page).

The existence of such a duplicate example conforms to a tradition by which knotted carpets were commonly woven in pairs. The intention may have been to show off these perfectly matching pieces end to end in a large chamber; or perhaps this was a step towards the rationalization of labour, for a single 'caller' could have dictated the instructions for wool colours and pattern changes to two teams of knotters simultaneously.

As in other carpets, the flowers are drawn with admirable precision. A skilled hand indeed was necessary to reproduce so many details with such perfection, bearing in mind that for each knot two strands of wool appear on the surface, and it is these strands that form the lines of such a delicate pattern.

MUGHAL CARPET

Date: early 17th century
Victoria and Albert Museum, London (T.403 – 1910)
Dimensions: 142.2×88.9 cm (56×35 in)
Asymmetrical knot:
926,300 knots per sq. metre (597 per sq. inch)
*   91 knots per 10 cm length (23 per inch length)*
*   102 knots per 10 cm width (26 per inch width)*
Warp of red, green and white silk
Weft of red silk
Wool pile

The ground of this carpet is in typical Mughal red, warm and limpid, which allows the pattern to be clearly seen. As in other rugs of the same origin, the light-coloured motifs, emphasized by some dark touches, stand out with luminous brilliance.

The field has the appearance of a lattice set before a flower urn. Were it real, such a grille would have been forged from iron in the West, but in the rich palaces of Jaipur it would have been made of some precious metal.

In the niches of this lattice are posies, each different from the others, arranged in the oriental manner and composed of stylized flowers: lilies, roses, irises, carnations and chrysanthemums. Although varied, the bouquets within the niches occupy the same volume, the smaller flowers having loosely spread foliage, the larger ones being more tightly arranged. This results in a varied yet balanced composition.

The border colours are the reverse of those in the field. On a light ground blossoming stems of red and green interlink. The border is channelled between two narrow guards, given substance by their small linear motifs.

This type of compartment design is also found on the carpet fragment in the collection of the Düsseldorf Kunstmuseum (see the previous page).

MUGHAL CARPET

Date: mid-17th century
Textile Museum, Washington, D.C. (R. 63.00.4)
Dimensions: 335×168 cm (132×66 in)
Asymmetrical knot:
241,800 knots per sq. metre (156 per sq. inch)
Cotton warp
Cotton weft
Wool pile

In India this type of carpet is called a lattice carpet. Many examples of this kind were woven during the Mughal period, and some very handsome fragments are preserved in museums of the United States.

The form of the lattice varies, as do the elements from which it is formed. Often the compartments are lozenges or eight-pointed stars as here. These are either outlined by gold thread, by very intricate red or gold branches, or even by elongated and curved lanceolate leaves, arranged to suit the requirements of the motif. Within the compartments are posies of three or five blooms, emerging from a vase, an urn or perhaps from a clump of foliage. Some are arranged back to back, others confronted or arranged in tiers.

The floral arrangements occupying this trellis are composed of bouquets of three flowers: tulips, roses, carnations, lotus blossoms or begonias. Their golden tones, subtly emphasized by the dark elements, become brilliant against the sparkling red of the field.

The ground of the border is the same colour as the field. The series of bouquets of three flowers in the border have as much variety as those on the field. Little red and beige flower buds pattern the guard stripes.

MUGHAL CARPET (detail)

Date: 17th century
Museum für Kunst und Gewerbe, Hamburg (1961.27)
Dimensions: 188×114 cm (74×45 in)
Asymmetrical knot:
1,566,000 knots per sq. metre (1,006 per sq. inch)
Warp of red, yellow, greenish-blue and white silk
Weft of red silk
Wool pile

The detail shown here illustrates a classic carpet of the Mughal period. Some examples in similar vein, but less finely knotted, are preserved in the collection of the Museum of the Shrine at Mashhad in Iran (see pp. 130-3).

The red ground colour is that found on the majority of Mughal carpets. Leafy floral scrolls of lozenge-shape form a trellis, the niches containing clusters of white flowers or a pink flower, alternatively.

The pale green border is a flower-bed of roses arranged with such unobtrusive symmetry that they appear to grow independently. This apparent freedom results in a very lively effect. Two light guard bands with garlands of carnations complete the frame.

VELVET MUGHAL CARPET

Date: 17th century
Metropolitan Museum of Art, New York (Purchase, 1927, Joseph Pulitzer Bequest: 27.115)
Dimensions: 466×259 cm (183×102 in)
Silk velvet weave on a satin ground with metal thread

This carpet is of indescribable beauty. Wherever the eye looks, on field or border, it is met with refinement of form and harmony of colouring. This carpet is woven like velvet, not knotted like a pile carpet. Its measurements and pattern suggest that is was intended to hang on a wall or in a tent like a tapestry.

It was probably woven in Kashmir, for its palette is that preferred by Kashmiri craftsmen. Moreover, such delicate work could only have been carried out by hands skilled in the weaving of fine shawls.

Large medallions with pendants form the traditional eight-pointed stars, outlined in red. Identical in structure, they contain arrangements of little flowers in various delightful colours: red, blue, pink, ivory and beige on a rose-pink ground. These medallions show a certain resemblance to those on the Ardebil Carpet in London.

The ivory border between two guards could be the work of a master-jeweller, so delicately minute are the tendrils and red flowers. A similar circular in-and-out effect of the scrolling can be found on other borders, but never with such elegance and delicacy.

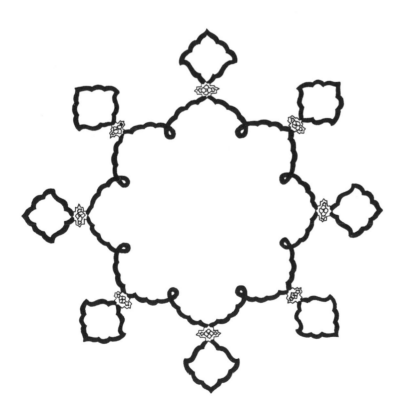

142

VELVET FLOORSPREAD (detail)

Date: 1650-1700
Keir Collection, London
Dimensions: 304×258 cm (120×102 in)
Velvet weave, in strips 70 to 72 cm (c. 28 in) in width

This carpet is skilfully composed; gently curved and elongated leaves, like ivory tusks, interlink with flowers to form large lozenges pinched in at the ends. The lozenges cover the whole surface of the red field and form a very intricate lattice. The centre of the lozenges is shared by two forms of delicate floral medallions: the inner one an eight-pointed star, the outer one with curvilinear surrounds. The medallions are focal points; graceful stems anchor them to pink and beige flowers that rise in tiers in ordered fashion inside the large lozenges. The arrangement of the motifs is harmonious, and their varied and understated colours diffuse a golden light.

The border holds more surprises. On a beige-brown ground, broad dark green leaves are arranged above and below big carnations in red and ivory, setting them off strongly.

The border is enclosed by triple guards: narrow red stripes with gold details or wider bands of ivory scattered with flowers with interlacing red stems and foliage unwinding like a garland.

ANTIQUE AGRA (restored)

Date: 18th century
Private collection
Dimensions: 257 × 238 cm (101 × 94 in)
Asymmetrical knot:
560,000 knots per sq. metre (361 per sq. inch)
*   70 knots per 10 cm length (18 per inch length)*
*   80 knots per 10 cm width (20 per inch width)*
Warp of 7 strands of undyed cotton
Weft of 7 strands of undyed cotton
Wool pile

In the colouring, the form of the motifs and the presence of animals, this carpet is redolent of the past and provides a feast for the eyes; however, while the red ground recalls the days of the Mughals, the composition places it within a later period.

This fine carpet is unfortunately not complete. Although the joins have been effected by an expert restorer, it is clear that motifs have been cut off both laterally and longitudinally. Many such masterpieces have been damaged in the past either by fire, water or rodents, some beyond recovery. We are fortunate that even this fragment has survived.

In the blue medallion with its saffron gold aureola are stems terminating in animal heads (birds in this instance)—a characteristic feature of Mughal patterns. Tigers and antelopes confront one another in the middle of the field on a red ground among flowers and palmettes. In the fragmentary green medallions, birds perch on the branches of rose bushes.

The saffron ground of the stately border provides a background for the leafy meander that winds around palmettes of red and green. All these motifs contain a smattering of delicate flowers. Two narrow bands of rosebuds edge the lateral borders only.

ANTIQUE AGRA

Date: end of the 18th century
Private collection
Dimensions: 198×124 cm (78×49 in)
Asymmetrical knot:
347,200 knots per sq. metre (224 per sq. inch)
* 62 knots per 10 cm length (16 per inch length)*
* 56 knots per 10 cm width (14 per inch width)*
Warp of 5 strands of undyed cotton
Weft of 4 strands of blue cotton
Wool pile

This carpet is a panorama of the flora and fauna of India, showing the full impact of the beauty and harshness of jungle life and the inexorable application of the laws of nature.

In the centre of the carpet is a claret-red square with scalloped edges, decorated with much delicacy. In its centre are flowers set like jewels to form a cross. All around are more flowers and birds, seemingly unconcerned by the accompanying hunting scenes.

On the field, leopards pursue ibexes, and tigers seize unlucky does in full flight. Stags stare at each other, not knowing where to flee. The spandrels are almost square, and on their pale green ground is a bird among flowers and pomegranates.

The border is formed from a succession of enchanting reciprocal bell-shaped motifs, which have much in common with those on the carpets of Isfahan that rank among the finest examples known.

ANTIQUE AGRA

Date: beginning of the 19th century
Private collection
Dimensions: 270 × 182 cm (106 × 72 in)
Asymmetrical knot:
490,000 knots per sq. metre (316 per sq. inch)
  70 knots per 10 cm length (18 per inch length)
  70 knots per 10 cm width (18 per inch width)
Warp of 12 strands of undyed cotton
Weft of red and undyed cotton
Wool pile

This rug is in a transitional style more closely related to the early carpets than to the modern ones. The central medallion recalls the Ardebil Carpet in the Victoria and Albert Museum, London, with its superimposed crosses and squares of unaffected style forming a motif with sixteen branches, drawn without exaggeration, with palmettes at each point: alternately eight dark and eight light palmettes. These form a corona for the medallion, adding volume and pointing outwards in all directions, providing a link with the other elements of the design.

Another unusual feature is that the stylized flowers of the medallion do not grow from vases in the middle of the borders but from standing or hanging oil-lamps. The designer must have wanted the centre of the carpet to be a theatre of light rather than a floral arrangement, and in this he succeeded, for the medallion explodes and scintillates on the flower-strewn blue ground.

The spandrels are similar in style to the central device and provide points of light in the corners of the field.

The border is a sequence of medallions: large-scale ones in red, the smaller ones in white framing a device rather like a Maltese cross. The two guards are very intricately knotted, especially the inner band with meanders winding around small flowers.

ANTIQUE AGRA (detail)

Date: 19th century
Private collection
Dimensions: 417×397 cm (164×156 in)
Asymmetrical knot:
200,000 knots per sq. metre (129 per sq. inch)
   50 knots per 10 cm length (13 per inch length)
   40 knots per 10 cm width (10 per inch width)
Warp of 8 strands of undyed cotton
Weft of pink and undyed cotton
Wool pile

From the detail reproduced, it can be seen that this is another very fine carpet, clearly of some age. The choice of motifs and warm colouring recall seventeenth-century examples, but this carpet is certainly later, as the colours indicate. The large-scale motifs can be readily deciphered without much close scrutiny of the pattern. Whether this is due to a concern for clarity and simplicity, or a sign that the artist had fallen victim to complacency, even decline, we cannot tell.

Whatever the reason, this carpet is still a magnificent piece that must have been woven to embellish the centre of some reception room in one of India's palaces.

The classic motifs of flowers, foliage and palmettes spread over the red ground. Those on the surrounding blue border are especially large, and it is this prominence rather than their variety that creates the effective frame for the field. The border is enclosed by six narrow guard bands.

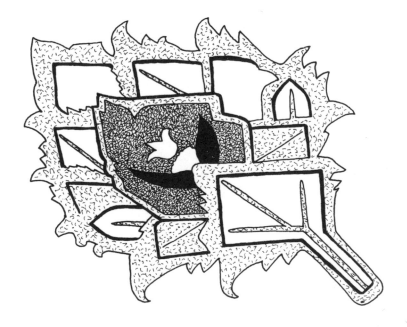

KASHMIR

Date: beginning of the 20th century
Private collection
Dimensions: 305 × 214 cm (120 × 84 in)
Asymmetrical knot:
435,200 knots per sq. metre (281 per sq. inch)
*   68 knots per 10 cm length (17 per inch length)*
*   64 knots per 10 cm width (16 per inch width)*
Warp of 2 strands of undyed silk
Weft of 3 strands of beige cotton
Silk pile

It is reasonable to assume that this remarkable piece was commissioned by some eminent person who sought an unusual specimen.

Boteh-miri motifs of amazingly elaborate structure provide the only decoration on the blue field. Large and of a different style from those on Iranian carpets, they are arranged in stepped formation, which gives a feeling of movement to the design.

The red border is covered with floral scrolls that freely overlap the two, light blue guards.

Although the colours are limited to eight, their warm tones—the reds and blues in particular—lend an exceptional brilliance to the silk, with sumptuous results.

KASHMIR

Date: 1936
Dimensions: 47×61 cm (18.5×24 in)
Asymmetrical knot:
3,300,000 knots per sq. metre (2,129 per sq. inch)
   220 knots per 10 cm length (56 per inch length)
   150 knots per 10 cm width (38 per inch width)
Warp of undyed silk
Weft of undyed silk
Silk pile

There have been many founders and reformers of spiritual movements in India, so that it is no simple matter to define the religious concepts of the country. On their priceless carpets Indian craftsmen have reproduced portraits of their philosophers—here, Cākyamuni, founder of Buddhism—or the features of the gods as they imagined them.

The emblem surmounting the parasol under which Cākyamuni stands is a monogram formed from the four initial letters of the Buddhist prayer: *Om, mani, padmē, hum.* It is estimated that the number of disciples of Buddhism in the world today is as many as three hundred million.

Buddhists believe in the eternal nature of the universe, which undergoes a series of mutations according to a pre-ordained law. The spirit of man evolves like the material world. Depending on the virtue or vice of a man's conduct, he oscillates between uplift and downfall. His purification is brought about through transmigrations, in the course of which he might be reincarnated in the body of an animal or fall, temporarily, into one of the eighteen Buddhist hells. When his vices are wiped away and virtue triumphs, his soul attains the state of Nirvana, a union with Ultimate Reality, characterized by the discovery of universal harmony in which all beings participate. Those who achieve perfection in this way become Bodhisattvas and, ultimately, Buddhas.

Four 'chosen' paths lead to perfection: knowledge; abstention from misconduct against one's fellow man; observation of the five prohibitions against stealing, killing, drunkenness, lying and adultery; and practice of the six virtues (giving alms, absolute morality, patience, goodness, vigour, charity).

KASHMIR

Date: 1936
Dimensions: 47×61 cm (18.5×24 in)
Asymmetrical knot:
3,840,000 knots per sq. metre (2,477 per sq. inch)
  240 knots per 10 cm length (61 per inch length)
  160 knots per 10 cm width (41 per inch width)
Warp of undyed silk
Weft of undyed silk
Silk pile

The Sanskrit text occupying the surround of the rug is the prayer addressed to the sun-god by his followers: 'I bow to Thee, Bhaskara (the Effulgent One, i.e., the sun-god), the repository of Dharma (righteousness), the proclaimer of virtuous actions and the Manifest God'.

Surya, the sun-god of Vedic mythology, is one of the most deeply venerated deities of India. The most sacred text of the Vedas, the *gayatri*, is dedicated to him. The Vedic texts, composed of four collections of verses, incantations and prayers, are the oldest texts in an Indo-European language and form the basis of the Vedic tradition of Hinduism. They are difficult to date precisely; the earliest are probably from around 1250 BC.

In this pattern, Surya, husband of Ushas, is depicted in his chariot, which is being drawn through the sky by a horse with seven heads. According to the legend, Aruna, the charioteer, is legless. In the centre of the upper border of the carpet, the emblem of the sun-god stands out clearly. The four symbols that Surya holds in his hands are the conch-shell (*shanka*), the origin of existence associated with heaven and the ocean; the wheel or the discus (*chakra*) representing creative thought; the club (*gada*), the power of knowledge; the lotus (*padma*), the image of the universe whence derives the law of perfection.

KASHMIR

Date: 1936
Dimensions: 47×60 cm (18.5×23.6 in)
Asymmetrical knot:
3,840,000 knots per sq. metre (2,477 per sq. inch)
  240 knots per 10 cm length (61 per inch length)
  160 knots per 10 cm width (41 per inch width)
Warp of undyed silk
Weft of undyed silk
Silk pile

Seated upon a lotus throne floating on the sea, this pattern shows Lakṣmī, goddess of beauty, grace, divine benevolence and prosperity.

In the centre of the upper border is the sacred symbol, *OM*. The text running around the carpet is a verse from the *Durgasaptashati* ('700 names of the Mother-Goddess'), a part of the *Markandeya Purāna*: 'I bow to Thee, Narayani (Lakṣmī), the Fair One (Gauri), the consort of the Three-Eyed One (Śiva), that bestows all happiness and welfare, that grants all desires and provides refuge to all'.

Lakṣmī is the wife of Vishnu (Viṣṇu). The incarnations, or avatars, of her husband determine the diversity of the names attributed to her. When Vishnu is manifest as Paraśurāma, she becomes Kalyam or Dhārani; for Krishna (Kṛṣṇa) she is Rukmini or Rādhā; for Rāma, Sītā.

But Lakṣmī is also invoked under other highly suggestive names: Chandchala, or Lola the Inconstant One; Śri goddess of Good Fortune; Hira the Precious One; Indira the Woman; Jaladhÿa, Daughter of the Ocean; Madhavi, Springtime; Kamal, or Padma, or even Padmavatī, the Lotus or Lotus-bearer. Lakṣmī is particularly worshipped during the important Festival of Lights (Dewali), held each year in October.

KASHMIR

Date: 1936
Dimensions: 47×61 cm (18.5×24 in)
Asymmetrical knot:
4,080,000 knots per sq. metre (2,632 per sq. inch)
*   240 knots per 10 cm length (61 per inch length)*
*   170 knots per 10 cm width (43 per inch width)*
Warp of undyed silk
Weft of undyed silk
Silk pile

The eighth avatar of Vishnu, Krishna, son of a king fostered out to cowherds as a child, is venerated by the lowly and ennobled by mystics. The highly coloured rustic adventures, pastoral flirtations, mischievous pranks and superhuman exploits of his boyhood and youth are related in the most lengthy epic known, the *Bhāgavata Purāna*. Krishna is often represented as a flute player bewitching sea-maidens or subduing the serpent Kaliya. Mystics interpret the adventures of Krishna as the quest for divine wisdom by souls thirsty for spiritual love.

In this carpet, Krishna is depicted as a cowherd, leaning against a tree laden with fruit in a garden of flowers. A peacock and some splendid birds perch on the tree's branches. Dressed in his yellow garment (the *pitamabara*), Krishna stands on the banks of the Yamuna River, on whose waters large birds are gently rocked. He sports a peacock feather on his forehead and clasps his flute in his hand. The temples and buildings of the city of Mathura are silhouetted on the far side of the river.

KASHMIR

Date: 1936
Dimensions: 48×61 cm (18.9×24 in)
Asymmetrical knot:
4,250,000 knots per sq. metre (2,741 per sq. inch)
   250 knots per 10 cm length (64 per inch length)
   170 knots per 10 cm width (43 per inch width)
Warp of undyed silk
Weft of undyed silk
Silk pile

The knotting of this example is incredibly fine. The knot-count is similar to those in the next two carpets illustrated. No other carpets in the world are known to reach this figure, for a knot-count of 1,000,000 per square metre (645 per square inch) would already be very fine, demanding highly skilled craftsmanship.

This carpet shows the seventh avatar of Vishnu: Rāma, son of Daśaratha, the king of Ayudhyā, and hero of the *Rāmāyana* epic, a favourite theme for temple decoration. Among other incidents depicted, a favourite one is Rāma's struggle against Rāvana, king of the demons, who abducted Rāma's wife, Sītā. His half-brother Lakśmana and the monkey-god Hanuman supported Rāma in his victorious combats. Here Sītā (daughter of Janaka, king of Videha) accompanics the hero, who is bearing his usual arms: a long bow and arrow.

KASHMIR

Date: 1936
Dimensions: 48×58 cm (18.9×22.8 in)
Asymmetrical knot:
4,250,000 knots per sq. metre (2,741 per sq. inch)
    250 knots per 10 cm length (64 per inch length)
    170 knots per 10 cm width (43 per inch width)
Warp of undyed silk
Weft of undyed silk
Silk pile

Ganeśa, the son of Śiva and Pārvatī, is one of the most ancient deities. He is incarnated in a human body with four arms and the head of an elephant. He also bears the name of Masterer of Obstacles (Vighnesha).

This carpet shows Ganeśa, and at his side, his two wives, Riddhi and Siddhi. In front of Ganeśa is his mount, a bandicoot (a rat as big as a cat), and his arm, the trident.

The explanation for the elephant's head on the shoulders of the god is given in the *Purānas*. Ganeśa once took it upon himself to disobey his father, Śiva. Instructed by his mother to stand guard before the room in which she was taking her bath, Ganeśa forebade Śiva himself to enter. The latter, maddened with rage, decapitated his son. But when he recovered from his anger, Śiva sent his people to search in the woods and bring back to him the head of the first living creature that they encountered. This turned out to be an elephant, and Śiva, in a hurry to make up for his unfortunate action, stuck the elephant's head forthwith upon his son's body.

KASHMIR

Date: 1936
Dimensions: 47 × 61 cm (18.5 × 24 in)
Asymmetrical knot:
4,250,000 knots per sq. metre (2,741 per sq. inch)
  250 knots per 10 cm length (64 per inch length)
  170 knots per 10 cm width (43 per inch width)
Warp of undyed silk
Weft of undyed silk
Silk pile

Śiva is one of the greatest gods of Hinduism. He is called Mahesha, Maheshvara and Shambu, the High God. Śiva is identified with the Vedic god Rudra and, in his terrible aspect, is termed the 'Destroyer'. Indeed, he embodies the redoubtable forces that rule the universe, the means by which nature destroys and renews itself indefinitely. Since renewal implies death and rebirth, Śiva is frequently held to possess creative as well as destructive powers, and his cult glorifies his fecundity. He is commonly worshipped in the form of the *lingam*, or symbolic phallus.

The celebrated bronzes of southern India depict Śiva as Nataraja, Lord of the Cosmic Dance, whose ritual gestures express his creative power and celebrate his victory over the demons of chaos. He is depicted in this role on this carpet, standing silhouetted in front of his abode, Mount Kailasa. The moon and the waters of the Ganges spring from Śiva's hair. Each stream is linked mysteriously with the primordial river of heavenly origin that also passes through his hair. A serpent encircles one of Śiva's arms, while his mount (a bull, Nandi the Joyous) lies at his side. The bull symbolizes generative power, which is subject to Śiva. It is the image of both the explosive forces of nature and instinct subdued by divine will.

KASHMIR

Date: 1936
Dimensions: 47 × 61 cm (18.5 × 24 in)
Asymmetrical knot:
3,300,000 knots per sq. metre (2,129 per sq. inch)
* 220 knots per 10 cm length (56 per inch length)*
* 150 knots per 10 cm width (38 per inch width)*
Warp of undyed silk
Weft of undyed silk
Silk pile

The Hindu deity Vishnu, one of the chief gods of Brahmanism, underwent a succession of incarnations, or *avataras*, in order to manifest himself in the tangible world. He is depicted in the shrines under these various forms; for example as the tortoise (Kurma), the man-lion (Narasimba) who fought and devoured a tyrant, the fish (Matsya), the boar (Varaha), the dwarf (Vamana) who revealed the greatness of God to an unbelieving king, and Paraśurāma (Rāma with the axe) who delivered the Brahmans from the oppression of the Kṣatriyas. The scriptures give 108 names to Vishnu: Srayambhu who exists of himself, Ananta the divine, Hari the abductor, Mukunda the liberator; Vishnu's most popular incarnation is the seventh: Rāma.

In this pattern Vishnu is shown reclining on the serpent Sheshanaga, sometimes called Anantashayanam. From the god's navel grows a lotus (*padma*) from which Brahmā or Chaturanana—the Supreme Being, the Creator, who is portrayed with four heads—was born.

KASHMIR

Date: 1936
Dimensions: 48×61 cm (18.9×24 in)
Asymmetrical knot:
3,300,000 knots per sq. metre (2,129 per sq. inch)
  220 knots per 10 cm length (56 per inch length)
  150 knots per 10 cm width (38 per inch width)
Warp of undyed silk
Weft of undyed silk
Wool pile

Śiva's consort is a goddess of many names. She is called Pārvatī, goddess of beauty and love, utterly devoted to the powerful Śiva. This is also the title she bears as mother of Ganeśa, or Ganapati, and of Kārttikeya, or Subrahmanya.

But she is also the dreaded Dūrga (the Inaccessible) or Kali (the Black One), patroness of thugs, shown here mounted upon a lion. In one of her many hands, Dūrga brandishes a sword, and in the other she clasps a lance with which she pierces the giant Mahisha, who is being devoured by her lion before her gaze. On either side of Dūrga are two representations of the Mother-Goddess: the first is Lakṣmī, goddess of wealth, gracefully bearing a lotus; and the second Sarasvatī, goddess of knowledge and the arts, playing on her lute *(vina)*. Before Dūrga stands Ganeśa, the elephant-headed deity, the god of war, who is bestriding a peacock. This image is inspired by the *Durgasaptashati*, part of the *Markandeya Purāna*.

KASHMIR (detail)

Date: 1980
Dimensions: 188×125 cm (74×49 in)
Asymmetrical knot:
576,000 knots per sq. metre (372 per sq. inch)
  80 knots per 10 cm length (20 per inch length)
  72 knots per 10 cm width (18 per inch width)
Warp of 3 strands of two-ply cotton
Weft of 2 strands of undyed cotton
Silk pile

This piece, of which only the centre detail is shown, is clearly a prayer rug, not merely because of its dimensions and the form of the field, but also because of details denoting a work of religious character. Indeed we seem to be looking at the niche of a mosque, crowned with ceramic tiles decorated with various motifs.

The arch is carried by two fragile columns resting on a particularly lively lower border. In the centre, a most delicate floral arrangement emerges from a very handsome vase, unfurling in successive sprays and filling the entire centre of the carpet. On either side of the vase is a garland of palmettes and flowers reaching the top of the niche. To the right and left of the vase lurk wild cats. They dare not attack the wading birds for their wings, beaks and feet are formidable weapons; however, the birds perched on the garland seem to intrigue them.

KASHMIR

Date: 1980
Dimensions: 182×118 cm (72×46 in)
Asymmetrical knot:
720,000 knots per sq. metre (464 per sq. inch)
  80 knots per 10 cm length (20 per inch length)
  90 knots per 10 cm width (23 per inch width)
Warp of 5 strands of two-ply silk
Weft of 3 strands of silk
Silk pile

This is a classic prayer rug. Above the *mihrab* runs an inscription, a verse from the Koran, probably: 'O God, You are great, and I have come before You to call upon Your name'. The field of this carpet, examined from top to bottom, seems to be covered with beings formed of flowers and foliage.

The spandrels are in two different styles: the upper ones forming the arch consist of indented red bands scattered with small pink and blue flowers; the lower ones, on a light ground, contain small beige and pink flowers caught in an intricate tracery of blue tendrils.

The same light ground appears on the border, which displays rose-pink meanders enclosing a series of large blue-centred brown flowers that alternate with three smaller ones. This border is enclosed by triple guard stripes, the central ones with pairs of beige and ivory flowers inlaid as though in a piece of marquetry.

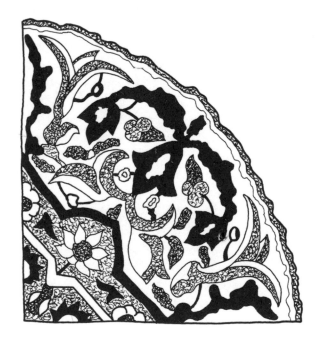

KASHMIR

Date: 1980
Dimensions: 212×180 cm (83×71 in)
Asymmetrical knot:
738,000 knots per sq. metre (476 per sq. inch)
90 knots per 10 cm length (23 per inch length)
82 knots per 10 cm width (21 per inch width)
Warp of 4 strands of undyed cotton
Weft of 2 strands of undyed cotton
Wool pile

Analysis of this carpet testifies clearly that present-day weavers have lost none of their skill. They are capable of creating pieces that lack none of the delicacy of early examples. Undoubtedly the colouring has evolved and the patterns have been adapted, but the genius remains.

The oval medallion is a model of refinement. It does not consist of a series of different base colours set within one another, as is usual. This medallion with its delicately wrought outline encloses scrolls developing over a pink ground and entwining small flowers. The centre of the medallion is a dark blue oval bearing a golden star; it stands in the middle of a pink flower-bed accented by rows of shimmering threads.

Around the medallion, antelopes of a species found only in India lead a joyful dance among flowers of varied form, under the interested gaze of crouching leopards which are depicted along the top and bottom of the field.

In the spandrels on a blue ground, oblivious to the excitement of the jungle below, birds of shimmering colours rest among flowers.

On the border stretches a chain of cartouches linked by rosettes. Thanks to the refinement of the pattern and the colours, the border is extremely rich. It is splendidly framed by eight bands, four on each side, simply striped with gold or with ribbons of flowers. Those adjacent to the border are evenly scattered with light-coloured flowers, large and small, that appear to be daisies.

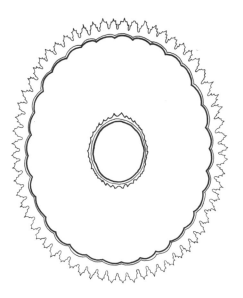

KASHMIR

Date: 1980
Dimensions: 179×126 cm (70×50 in)
Asymmetrical knot:
640,000 knots per sq. metre (413 per sq. inch)
   80 knots per 10 cm length (20 per inch length)
   80 knots per 10 cm width (20 per inch width)
Warp of 4 strands of undyed cotton
Weft of 4 strands of undyed cotton
Wool and silk pile

Only expert and particularly fine knotting could have produced a carpet as perfect as this prayer rug—a masterpiece of mellow colours and detailing.

The cream-coloured ground of the *mihrab* is in silk; on either side of the *mihrab* is an ornate pillar resting on a pedestal surrounded by flowers.

A bouquet of flowering branches scrolls upwards from a vase at the base of the *mihrab*; there is a stylized tree on both sides of the vase. The rest of the field is covered with flowers; those growing along the ground are tall stemmed. The spandrels have red grounds and are strewn with a large flower and a single flowering tendril.

Palmettes and flowering scrolls decorate the border, which is contained with grace and discretion between two bands filled with lovely little roses.

KASHMIR

Date: 1980
Dimensions: 142×90 cm (56×35 in)
Asymmetrical knot:
850,000 knots per sq. metre (548 per sq. inch)
100 knots per 10 cm length (25 per inch length)
85 knots per 10 cm width (22 per inch width)
Warp of 4 strands of undyed cotton
Weft of 2 strands of blue and undyed cotton
Wool and silk pile

This rug is distinguished by the soft palette so beloved of modern Kashmiri weavers and by the curvaceous forms of the floral patterns and the fan-shaped plumage of the birds.

In the upper corners two winged creatures—probably peacocks in flight—spread their majestic feathers of blue, red and gold.

The centre of the carpet might be regarded as a simple medallion from which grow elegant sprays of blossoming stems that fall along the sides, but it might also be taken for a stylized peacock spreading its tail. The dark blue medallion terminating in a point would represent the peacock's head and beak and the flowering branches spreading overhead in fan shape, its tail. In the centre of the lower border stands a vase containing a fan-shaped arrangement of flowers, again rather like a peacock's tail. In short, this bird seems to have provided the theme for the entire design.

On either side of the vase grow clusters of flowers in light beige, cream and blue, each surmounted by a little bird.

The border is a dark blue band bearing an arrangement of ivory palmettes with pink and gold centres, linked by the branches of small ochre flowers. Double guards frame the border: the inner one forming a more stately garland, the outer one with wreaths of small golden flowers on an ivory ground.

KASHMIR (detail)

Date: 1980
Dimensions: 260×183 cm (102×72 in)
Asymmetrical knot:
525,600 knots per sq. metre (339 per sq. inch)
*   72 knots per 10 cm length (18 per inch length)*
*   73 knots per 10 cm width (19 per inch width)*
Warp of 5 strands of undyed cotton
Weft of 2 strands of blue cotton
Wool pile

The detail opposite comes from a so-called medallion carpet. The central motif, isolated on the blue pile of the field, is like a skilfully worked gem. In this instance, however, let us consider an area of the carpet that is not always favoured with a detailed description, even though it may be just as intricate as the central medallion—the spandrels and the bands around them.

First of all, note the elegance with which the spandrels stand out against the ground-colour of the field. The curved outlines with details fashioned like wrought metal accentuate the impression that we are looking at a piece of jewellery. On the rose-coloured ground is a shower of small red, blue and gold flowers surrounding an angular arabesque on a gold ground.

Like the ground of the spandrel, the dark blue ground of the border is strewn with innumberable small red, sky-blue and gold flowers. This exuberance serves to emphasize the talent of the artist and his weavers.

There are four guard bands around the floral border. Each bears a pattern of perfectly ordered flowers. Those adjacent to the border are on a gold ground, the outer ones on a sky-blue ground.

KASHMIR

Date: 1980
Dimensions: 178×116 cm (70×46 in)
Asymmetrical knot:
560,000 knots per sq. metre (362 per sq. inch)
*   70 knots per 10 cm length (18 per inch length)*
*   80 knots per 10 cm width (20 per inch width)*
Warp of 4 strands of undyed cotton
Weft of 6 strands of undyed cotton
Wool and silk pile

The pattern of this prayer rug is very curious. The flower sprays do not grow out of a vase set on the lower border. Instead they spread from the base of the carpet in successive waves, like a fir-tree.

The branches—some slender, others thick, curling like a ribbon—are not lost among foliage and flowers (palmettes, sunflowers and others) strewn over the golden field of the carpet. They constitute a most handsome linear pattern in the centre of the carpet.

At the base of the field, clusters of sky-blue flowers in spike formation, together with lanceolate, curved leaves pointing outwards to the lateral borders, provide the key to the design.

The upper area of the field is ringed by two scrolls bearing a network of foliage and flowers on a grey-blue ground, which set off the top of the arch and the border.

On the cream-coloured border stretches a garland of palmettes containing, in the centre, a motif strangely akin to a human face, interlinked by a species of flower that can also be seen on some carpet fragments preserved in collections in the United States, with their petals replaced by a bird's head. On the red ground of the two guard bands runs a chain of charming gold and blue flower buds.

KASHMIR

Date: 1980
Dimensions: 185×121 cm (73×48 in)
Asymmetrical knot:
640,000 knots per sq. metre (413 per sq. inch)
* 80 knots per 10 cm length (20 per inch length)*
* 80 knots per 10 cm width (20 per inch width)*
Warp of 5 strands of undyed cotton
Weft of 5 strands of undyed cotton
Wool and silk pile

The remarkable feature of this prayer rug is not the form or composition of its central motif, a vase containing a floral arrangement that expands over the light ground up to the apex of the scalloped arch, typical of prayer rugs. Its merit derives rather from the fineness of the knotting, which makes it possible to depict the tiniest motifs with greater precision than a pencil can draw.

Even the most minute flowers springing from the vase and emerging from the grass along the lower border are reproduced to perfection. Thus the field becomes a riot of flowers, indeed a riot of colours from tulips, roses, carnations, lotus blossoms, irises, clusters of campanulas and other enchanting small flowers. Six birds pose discreetly yet clearly on flowering branches, apparently rendered mute by the surfeit of beauty.

The dark blue border is uncommon in focussing all light onto the field. On the wide band, the crowd of palmettes and scrolls sometimes seem to take on mask-like features.

KASHMIR

Date: 1980
Dimensions: 93×61 cm (37×24 in)
Asymmetrical knot:
720,000 knots per sq. metre (464 per sq. inch)
  90 knots per 10 cm length (23 per inch length)
  80 knots per 10 cm width (20 per inch width)
Warp of 4 strands of undyed cotton
Weft of 4 strands of undyed cotton
Silk pile

This carpet is comparable to a painting by a great artist. And, indeed, it is possible that the designer is such a person. The composition is free; its harmony does not derive from the symmetry of its lines or the position of its motifs. Through the medium of a single plant, the designer has succeeded in endowing his work with an incomparable equilibrium, depicting flowers and foliage in varying stages of growth and controlling contrasts with a consummate art.

This is not a floral arrangement but a real, natural, unembellished bush. Only certain features and colours have been emphasized (the browns of the branches and large leaves), while the colouring of the flowers and lesser foliage has been subdued so as to enliven the whole. Certain almost imperceptible subtleties of line and tone can be picked out in the small details of the carpet—a result that can only be achieved by the use of extremely fine knotting.

The border, generously ornamented with quintuple clusters of buds in red, green, blue, pink and brown, provides a fitting frame for this exceptionally beautiful composition.

KASHMIR

Date: 1980
Dimensions: 136×126 cm (54×50 in)
Asymmetrical knot:
640,000 knots per sq. metre (413 per sq. inch)
  80 knots per 10 cm length (20 per inch length)
  80 knots per 10 cm width (20 per inch width)
Warp of 3 strands of two-ply undyed cotton
Weft of 3 strands of two-ply undyed cotton
Wool pile

This carpet, woven without a border, is original in several respects.

The almost square central motif is inscribed within a serrated gold frame. Displaying a network etched with beige and brown tendrils on a dark ground, it contains a brown circle around which an inscription winds. Then, right in the centre and set off by the preceding motifs, a black spot is set like an onyx in a piece of jewellery.

The medallions in the corners, embellished with lilies, are surmounted by winged personages derived from Indian mythology. The small twin medallions flanking the central motif seem to be supported by two graceful S-shaped white bands, called 'cloudbands'.

Finally, the branches that line the field, bearing flowers and foliage, terminate in animal heads. These motifs were inspired by a Mughal carpet of the seventeenth century, a fragment of which is in the collection of the Musée des Arts décoratifs in Paris.

KASHMIR

Date: 1980
Dimensions: 214×150 cm (84×59 in)
Asymmetrical knot:
756,000 knots per sq. metre (488 per sq. inch)
  90 knots per 10 cm length (23 per inch length)
  84 knots per 10 cm width (21 per inch width)
Warp of 3 strands of undyed cotton
Weft of 2 strands of undyed cotton
Wool and silk pile

Those who have a preference for soft colouring will admire this lovely, finely knotted piece, strewn with decorative elements of extreme delicacy. In the centre of the pink field, the medallion is formed of two eight-pointed stars filled with diminutive bouquets of flowers. The inner star almost matches the contours of the outer one but has a lighter ground.

In the middle of each of the borders a small fan-shaped arrangement of blue and white flowers bursts from a flower-pot. Elongated palmettes, with cypress-like silhouettes oriented towards the medallion, surround the pot. Sprays of flowers held in place by tendril scrolls spread over the bi-coloured ground of the spandrels, which is pale green in front, receding to bluish-green in the corners.

The border, bounded by two triple guard bands, is a sequence of two alternating floral motifs ornamented with tiny flowers in blue, red and pink.

KASHMIR

Date: 1980
Dimensions: 196 × 117 cm (77 × 46 in)
Asymmetrical knot:
640,000 knots per sq. metre (413 per sq. inch)
  80 knots per 10 cm length (20 per inch length)
  80 knots per 10 cm width (20 per inch width)
Warp of 4 strands of undyed cotton
Weft of 2 strands of undyed cotton
Wool pile

The design of this piece could be the work of a jeweller, and certainly the hands that tied these knots are as skilled as those that make the finest jewellery. The undulating and crinkled edge of this medallion also appears in modern goldsmith's work.

Within the medallion, leafy green fronds bearing blue and white flowers swirl elegantly on the pink ground.

On the field, a network of brown cloudbands shrouds the medallion, and beyond them, among flowering shrubs, brown bears chase the blue does romping around the medallion. At a distance in the spandrels, birds perched on slender branches follow the revels of the wild animals.

The border motifs—large medallions with rounded edges that alternate with flowers—are inspired by seventeenth-century models. The two guard bands contain a series of tiny blue and white flowers on a red ground.

KASHMIR

Date: 1980
Dimensions: 178×122 cm (70×48 in)
Asymmetrical knot:
490,000 knots per sq. metre (316 per sq. inch)
* 70 knots per 10 cm length (18 per inch length)*
* 70 knots per 10 cm width (18 per inch width)*
Warp of 4 stands of undyed cotton
Weft of 2 strands of undyed cotton
Silk pile

There is much mysticism in the compositions of oriental carpets. Perhaps the intention of the designer was to transport the owner of this carpet to a paradisial world of fruits and flowers, where the spirit finds sustenance and joy.

At the base of the field the mountains of Kashmir are arranged, their peaks directed towards heaven. Two tall trees serve as reminders that all life strives to rejoin the heights whence it came.

Two tree trunks emerging from the mountains support a vase containing a mitre-shaped arrangement of flowers and foliage, some so finely worked as to be barely distinguishable. Above the vase the two trunks reappear, subdividing into branches to accompany the bouquet, then drawing together and finally dispersing, bearing flowers and fruit that spread over the entire upper part of the field.

The border has a ground only slightly darker than that of the field, and runs between two floral bands that boldly frame the unusual pattern of large and small palmettes accompanied by single flowers.

KASHMIR

Date: 1980
Dimensions: 275×217 cm (108×85 in)
Asymmetrical knot:
810,000 knots per sq. metre (522 per sq. inch)
  90 knots per 10 cm length (23 per inch length)
  90 knots per 10 cm width (23 per inch width)
Warp of 3 strands of two-ply undyed cotton
Weft of undyed cotton
Wool pile

This carpet gives an impression of clarity, lightness and great refinement. Its design, typical of Kashmir, recalls the famous shawls of that country. It is an airy composition; motifs employed, although subtle, are set out without mystery—an example of 'draughtmanship' of the highest order.

The central lozenge needs a clear field around it so that the elegance of the branches forming its structure, weighed down with flowers and foliage, do not suffer from the proximity of other patterns. The same applies to the flowering branches springing from the corners of the field and encircling it with stems, foliage and red and blue flowers, all executed with the same delicate touch, and which no other element must be allowed to overwhelm.

The border is composed of only two bands and is patterned with an array of branches that coil round to form palmettes and flowers identical to those on the other devices but which are arranged more closely here, so that the border is reinforced and forms a sturdy framework.

KASHMIR

Date: 1980
Dimensions: 183×126 cm (72×50 in)
Asymmetrical knot:
640,000 knots per sq. metre (413 per sq. inch)
* 80 knots per 10 cm length (20 per inch length)*
* 80 knots per 10 cm width (20 per inch width)*
Warp of 4 strands of undyed cotton
Weft of undyed cotton
Wool pile

The pattern covering this carpet is a typical Kashmiri creation, reminiscent of the traditional shawls of the country.

In composition, however, it is not at all common. Striped with longitudinal bands of varying widths, the carpet's field bears light stripes with a chain of dark motifs and dark stripes scattered with light ones.

The designer has achieved an extraordinarily successful result: he has animated this carpet with a single motif, freely repeated on both field and borders. This motif is the *boteh-miri*, or princely flower, which is also found on Persian carpets, but which originated in India. Varying in size, direction and colour, it covers the entire field without giving the slightest impression of fastidious uniformity. The skilful mix of colours contributes to the success of the result.

The extra borders that terminate both ends are also an original feature. Formed of broken arches sheltering flowering plants, they restrain perfectly the tendency of the design to spread in a lengthwise direction.

KASHMIR

Date: 1980
Dimensions: 208 × 141 cm (82 × 56 in)
Asymmetrical knot:
640,000 knots per sq. metre (413 per sq. inch)
*   80 knots per 10 cm length (20 per inch length)*
*   80 knots per 10 cm width (20 per inch width)*
Warp of 3 strands of two-ply undyed cotton
Weft of 4 strands of undyed cotton
Wool pile

Clearly this carpet has been conceived solely to allow the extremely finely knotted central medallion, already highlighted by its blue ground and individual border, to express all its richness, just as a chased gold mount might provide a setting for a sapphire.

The medallion contains a vase and bouquet from which clusters of small, minutely detailed flowers spray out in all directions. With its oval border flooded with tiny flowers scattered over a dark red ground, this carpet calls to mind miniatures in early manuscripts.

On the field of the carpet, around the central device, *boteh-miri* motifs swirl elegantly, forming a ravishing mosaic.

The border is a path of dark blue, bearing a procession of bunches of five or six completely classic flowers. Twin guard stripes of flowers on a golden ground surround it.

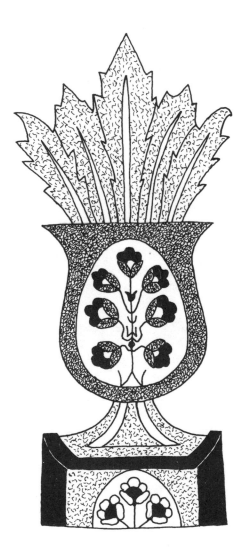

KASHMIR

Date: 1980
Dimensions: 137 × 129 cm (54 × 51 in)
Asymmetrical knot:
810,000 knots per sq. metre (522 per sq. inch)
*   90 knots per 10 cm length (23 per inch length)*
*   90 knots per 10 cm width (23 per inch width)*
Warp of 3 strands of two-ply undyed cotton
Weft of 3 strands of two-ply undyed cotton
Wool pile

This rug, a veritable woven painting, seems to synthesize the customs and beliefs of Kashmir.

In the central medallion, a scalloped disc of gold, are three men. Two of them are clasping a sabre in one hand and shield in the other, fighting a duel. The third, standing back watchfully, seems to act as referee. At their feet a small dog, standing on his hindlegs, barks at the fighting men. This is a remarkable piece of observation, for no dog can help reacting to the noises of a fight.

On the other hand, the bird, perched on the tree under which the sword-play is staged, follows the fight with an impassive gaze.

Around the central medallion on the warm red field revolve the classic motifs of the jungle: flowering branches through which wild beasts, game and domestic animals battle their way.

On the single guard band are eight small medallions containing women playing various musical instruments, Muses probably, whose sweet melodies attempt to quell

the violence on earth. These medallions are separated by cartouches inscribed with texts.

On the border, which extends to the edges of the rug, small red medallions, also bearing inscriptions whose meanings are not clear, are decorated and interlinked by arabesques.

206

KASHMIR

Date: 1980
Dimensions: 201×124 cm (79×49 in)
Asymmetrical knot:
640,000 knots per sq. metre (413 per sq. inch)
  80 knots per 10 cm length (20 per inch length)
  80 knots per 10 cm width (20 per inch width)
Warp of 3 strands of two-ply silk
Silk weft
Silk pile

The *boteh-miri*, or princely flower, is the only motif used in the composition of this design. Its oblong shape, narrowed and pinched at one end, and its flexibility permit such repetition, with the *boteh-miri* motifs coiling around and encircling each other, then separating and regaining their separate identity.

A wonderful mosaic is the foundation of this carpet. In using greens next to blues, the designer took a calculated risk. The subtlety with which these two colours are handled and the mellowness accentuated by the insertion of pale pink contribute to its success.

The same motif occurs in more compact form in the border, woven in the same shades, but here it runs between two double guards that prevent the colours from merging and do not detract from the visual impact of the field.

KASHMIR

Date: 1980
Dimensions: 196×135 cm (77×53 in)
Asymmetrical knot:
490,000 knots per sq. metre (316 per sq. inch)
*   70 knots per 10 cm length (18 per inch length)*
*   70 knots per 10 cm width (18 per inch width)*
Warp of 3 strands of two-ply undyed cotton
Weft of 4 strands of undyed cotton
Wool and silk pile

The pale blue border is carefully framed by two guard bands to separate the colour of the inner band from that of the field.

The border is strewn with detached flowers, scattered liberally and naturalistically, and houses wonderful little birds, beaks poised, that seem to await the passing of some insect—an image of the tranquil beauty of the Kashmiri countryside.

In the flower carpets already shown, the bouquet usually takes shape at the base of the field. It springs upwards from a vase in sprays that spread all over the surface. In this carpet, however, the posies spring from the centre of the field and from the central point of the borders, converging to give the design perfect harmony, combined with a certain symmetry.

In the centre is a sunflower symbolizing the sun. Beyond, towards either end, sprays of flowers in fan-tail formation burst from two stylized vases standing on a light field. Two other bouquets growing from the sunflower expand towards the lateral borders.

An unusual feature is apparent in the two vases resting on the longitudinal borders; they contain sprays directed towards the centre of the carpet, so that the flowers from the sun merge with those from the borders. These flowers of all species and colours, with stems interlinking harmoniously, adorn the rose-coloured ground of the carpet.

KASHMIR

Date: 1980
Dimensions: 104×82 cm (40.9×32.3 in)
Asymmetrical knot:
640,000 knots per sq. metre (413 per sq. inch)
  80 knots per 10 cm length (20 per inch length)
  80 knots per 10 cm width (20 per inch width)
Warp of 4 strands of undyed cotton
Weft of 4 strands of undyed cotton
Silk and wool pile with gold threads

Since the craft of carpet weaving has spread throughout most countries of the East over the centuries, it is quite natural that motifs proper to one country should also appear in the patterns of another. This is especially true of Persian rhomboids and arabesques, which are widely used.

This carpet, however, is an exception, for there are no foreign elements in either the field, borders or guard bands. All over it there are flowers native to Kashmir; these are unlike any found elsewhere and are of every variety and hue.

This carpet can be likened to a relatively small painting set within a massive frame that gives it the necessary depth. There are three borders, one of which is very wide; they run between four light, finely decorated guards and form the frame for the carpet. In the centre, the floral arrangement that springs from a very elegant vase has clear outlines, is well-proportioned and dense; the stems are strong and the flowers fully open. If placed in a well-lit position, this powerfully framed bouquet should sparkle on its dark ground, for its treasury of brilliant colours is picked out with gold thread.

KASHMIR

Date: 1980
Dimensions: 184×120 cm (72×47 in)
Asymmetrical knot:
525,000 knots per sq. metre (339 per sq. inch)
  75 knots per 10 cm length (19 per inch length)
  70 knots per 10 cm width (18 per inch width)
Warp of 3 strands of three-ply undyed cotton
Weft of 2 strands of undyed cotton
Silk pile

It is hardly surprising that the natural treasures of Kashmir are featured on Kashmiri carpets: sprays of flowers with birds clinging to them, bursting from wonderfully fashioned vases. Kashmir is, *par excellence*, the country of flowers and birds. Flowers are everywhere, in gardens, meadows and homes, where they are the most popular form of decoration. Their colours—often in the gentlest of tones—charm the beholder and calm the spirit. Similarly, there is an infinite variety of birds in Kashmir. They pass without fear wherever their will takes them. Man holds no terror for them, a fact that often surprises visitors to the country.

With this in mind this pattern is self-explanatory. Flowers emerge from a vase at the base of the field and twist up towards the top of the carpet. Some push up through the centre, while the supple stems of others, borne down by the weight of birds, climb the sides to meet at the top of the field.

The heavily accentuated border, which runs between triple guards, is sprinkled with flowers and leaves similar to those in the spandrels on the upper corners of the field. The genuineness of this carpet derives from its soft colouring and from the authenticity of its motifs.

KASHMIR

Date: 1980
Dimensions: 358×273 cm (141×107 in)
Asymmetrical knot:
684,000 knots per sq. metre (441 per sq. inch)
  90 knots per 10 cm length (23 per inch length)
  76 knots per 10 cm width (19 per inch width)
Warp of 4 strands of undyed cotton
Weft of 3 strands of undyed cotton
Wool and silk pile

Hunting scenes are found only very rarely on the rugs of Kashmir; the people of this country love animals too deeply to choose this pastime as a favourite theme. This carpet, however, represents the inevitable exception to the tradition; moreover, it differs greatly from those of other regions that depict hunting parties.

There are a great number of riders in this pattern. Men and horses, scattered among the trees, are poised in various attitudes, which result in a very animated effect. The hunters hold in their hands either a bow, a sabre or a lance—the traditional weapon of Kashmir. Lions, tigers, stags and does form the prey whose bounding movements, whether fleeing their aggressors or turning to face them, stamp the carpet with a harmony derived from power and grace.

The floral borders, composed of remarkably delicate garlands on a pastel-rose ground, are final proof that the author of this inventive work was inspired by the early miniatures and traditional motifs of his country.

KASHMIR

Date: 1980
Dimensions: 104×82 cm (41×32 in)
Asymmetrical knot:
624,000 knots per sq. metre (402 per sq. inch)
*   78 knots per 10 cm length (19 per inch length)*
*   80 knots per 10 cm width (20 per inch width)*
Warp of 4 strands of undyed cotton
Weft of 2 strands of undyed cotton
Silk and wool pile

Astonishing features that spring to life with great intensity may emerge when a carpet is scrutinized minutely. A flower, tiny but of scintillating brilliance, suddenly stands out amidst its neighbours; a bird with an open beak seems to sing its joy in living in this flowered bed. Suggestive new forms are continually taking shape; here, for example, the top of the bouquet in the field takes on the appearance of a lion's head with almond eyes and a mane that is simulated by the outspread wings of two large birds.

All the characteristics of Kashmiri carpets are embodied in this piece: the great number and position of the flowers, the birds filling both border and field, and the pale pink colouring. Indeed, this was the intention of the young designer from Srinagar.

Two fairly wide guard bands, with delicate interlaced arabesques, restrain the border. The gentle tones of the pattern and its structure are evidence of the modern revival of the Kashmiri carpet.

KASHMIR

Date: 1980
Dimensions: 187×122 cm (73.6×48 in)
Asymmetrical knot:
525,000 knots per sq. metre (339 per sq. inch)
70 knots per 10 cm length (18 per inch length)
75 knots per 10 cm width (19 per inch width)
Warp of 3 strands of three-ply undyed cotton
Weft of 2 strands of undyed cotton
Silk pile

Words cannot convey the beauty of this almost perfect prayer rug, characterized by harmony of composition, unity of colouring and elegance of motifs.

The central feature is a vase from which sprays of flowers of many forms and colours burst like fireworks. Some are discreetly elegant and enhance the intensity of the others' brilliance.

This sumptuous posy rests on a scalloped ogival *mihrab* with a clear, cream-coloured ground. The effect produced is that of a stained-glass window with a predominantly floral theme. The dark ground at the peak of the ogive contrasts with the light field within, giving it increased force. In the corners two motifs containing three flowers are traced. Their position and implied strength likcn thcm to the capitals of two buttresses supporting the framework.

The latter is a broad border, a waterway reflecting the sky, through which run a series of floral scrolls interlaced in perfect harmony. The restrained tones highlight the clarity of the central area of the carpet.

KASHMIR

Date: 1980
Dimensions: 188×123 cm (74×48.4 in)
Asymmetrical knot:
738,000 knots per sq. metre (476 per sq. inch)
  90 knots per 10 cm length (23 per inch length)
  82 knots per 10 cm width (21 per inch width)
Warp of 4 strands of undyed cotton
Weft of 2 strands of undyed cotton
Wool and silk pile

Some rugs featured in this book are designed horizontally, rather like an arrow pointing towards a holy place. Others are designed vertically, as here, and convey an impression of an ascent, an impulse towards heaven reminiscent of the peaks of Kashmir whence they derive, by means of the form of the central motif as well as by the peaked border at the top. Because they have an obvious upper and lower part, such carpets can be displayed to advantage either hung on a wall or spread out on the floor of a room.

The connoisseur of oriental carpets would find the design and colour of this example unusual, for the designer has sought to give it a new structure and colouring, while respecting traditional patterns.

The central pattern of a vase with flowering branches in harmonious curves is remarkable for the extreme delicacy of the elements of which it is composed. Although this design recalls the *mille-fleurs* patterns of the Mughals, its pastel tones are undoubtedly typical of Kashmir and perfectly suited to present-day interiors.

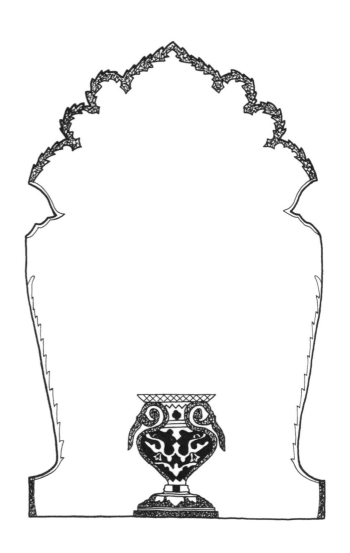

KASHMIR

Date: 1980
Dimensions: 215 × 140 cm (85 × 55 in)
Asymmetrical knot:
640,000 knots per sq. metre (413 per sq. inch)
   80 knots per 10 cm length (20 per inch length)
   80 knots per 10 cm width (20 per inch width)
Warp of 3 strands of three-ply undyed cotton
Weft of undyed cotton
Silk pile

This carpet reminds us of the wonderful prayer rugs of the seventeenth century, but the exquisite softness of the colour scheme, the large flowers and the absence of strapwork identify it as a creation of the present day. It demonstrates the genius of the designers of modern Kashmir, who preserve the essence of ancestral patterns, adapting them to meet present-day demands.

Conforming to tradition, the flowers covering the pale blue field rise and spread from a central vase and the two tree trunks that accompany it. These large, highly detailed specimens meet at the top of the field as if to shelter an oil-lamp suspended from the apex of the ogive. For the faithful at prayer, this lamp is not only a reminder of the presence of the divinity but also the symbol of the lucid and fervent nature of prayer itself.

The brown hillocks undulating along the lower border suggest the mountains of Kashmir or the earth whence all life springs.

On the border's ochre ground is a veritable floral festival, with a multitude of small flower clusters in various colours, between palmettes and scrolls. The motifs on the two guard bands could represent butterflies with outspread wings, for those creatures are much in evidence in Kashmir.

KASHMIR

Date: 1980
Dimensions: 165×90 cm (65×35 in)
Asymmetrical knot:
560,000 knots per sq. metre (361 per sq. inch)
   80 knots per 10 cm length (20 per inch length)
   70 knots per 10 cm width (18 per inch width)
Warp of 3 strands of two-ply undyed cotton
Weft of undyed cotton
Wool pile

This carpet is a runner with narrow stripes ranged alongside each other, to lend depth to the design and lead the eye agreeably towards other, distant things.

The bands are designed in groups of three. The last of the three is a clear, translucent beige, patterned with detached red roses, placed at some distance from each other. These provide decorative interest on the light field, while leaving sufficient space for its full lightening effect to be diffused over the remainder of the darker areas of the carpet. The other two stripes display an identical, predominantly green motif. Red flowers, too, are evident, trapped in the scrolls of leafy fronds that provide cohesion to the pattern. The final band, of ochre colour, is distinctly darker than its partners.

The narrow, ribbon-like bands separating and framing the broader stripes are scattered with small flowers: the red ones with blue-centred beige blossoms, and the blue ones with red-centred beige flowers.

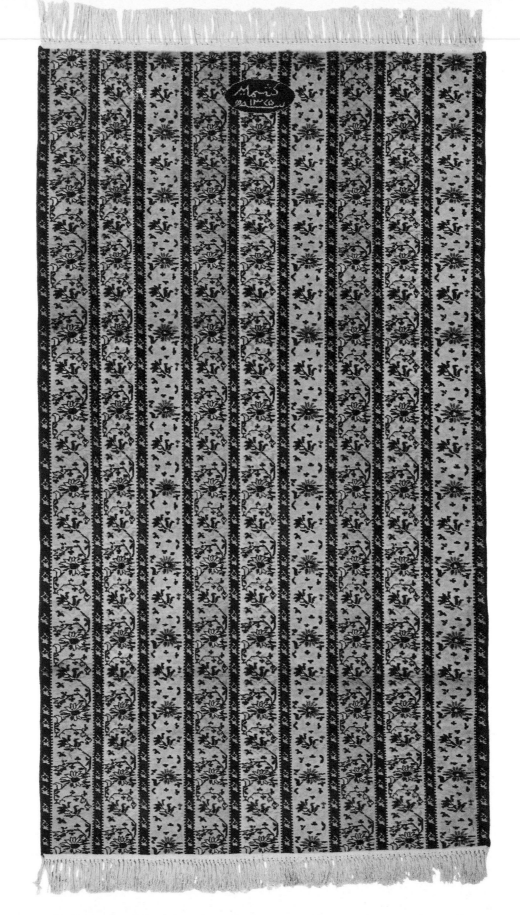

KASHMIR

Date: 1980
Dimensions: 211×153 cm (83×60 in)
Asymmetrical knot:
680,000 knots per sq. metre (439 per sq. inch)
    80 knots per 10 cm length (20 per inch length)
    85 knots per 10 cm width (22 per inch width)
Warp of 3 strands of undyed cotton
Weft of 2 strands of undyed cotton
Silk pile

In this carpet, with its greatly enlarged medallion unfolding for us to admire, the profound links that exist between certain crafts—carpet weaving, stained glass and jewellery—are clearly in evidence. This finely wrought eight-pointed star, set with a dark blue octagon with small flower buds sparkling like diamonds, could just as well be a component of a jewelled pendant or a rose window in a cathedral.

The blue octagon is surrounded by a network of volutes bearing flowers, foliage and palmettes. Each of the eight points houses two large birds, pelicans apparently, in confronted stance, separated by a floral spray.

In the field lions leap upon antelopes, seizing them in their jaws. These scenes of violence in nature, quite normal in the jungle, unfold on a setting of wonderful flowers in blue, white, brown, beige and pinkish tones—the soft hues beloved of today's carpet designers in Kashmir.

In the border, pairs of antelopes, birds and other animals are relaxing on the blue-black ground.

KASHMIR (detail)

Date: 1980
Dimensions: 182×125 cm (72×49 in)
Asymmetrical knot:
490,000 knots per sq. metre (316 per sq. inch)
  70 knots per 10 cm length (18 per inch length)
  70 knots per 10 cm width (18 per inch width)
Warp of 4 strands of undyed cotton
Weft of undyed cotton
Wool pile

This striking carpet conveys an impression of order and strength, tempered by gentle tones of soft blue and beige. The carpet is covered by a lattice composed of lozenges, created by the alignment of the motifs on the blue-black field. No branches or scrolls exist to form its outlines. The motifs are highly stylized sprays in small vases, arranged in strictly alternating rows: red ones followed by blue and beige ones, their colouring moderating the red. Small beige leaves, emphasized by the dark ground, separate the bouquets.

The border is much more intricate. It is embellished with a succession of sprigs of various flowers in clusters of five or seven—some in slender vases, others in urns—on a red ground. The arched form of the diminutive motifs in the two guard bands creates an enchanting festoon effect.

KASHMIR

Date: 1980
Dimensions: 134×85 cm (53×33 in)
Asymmetrical knot:
950,000 knots per sq. metre (613 per sq. inch)
 100 knots per 10 cm length (25 per inch length)
 95 knots per 10 cm width (24 per inch width)
Warp of 4 strands of white and beige silk
Weft of 3 strands of white silk
Silk pile

The male figure with black beard, whose red tunic belted with gold stands out against the blue field of the carpet, is the Mughal emperor Jahangir, son of Akbar, who reigned from 1605 to 1627. In his hands Jahangir holds a lotus flower that gleams like a sceptre. Flowers do not crowd the carpet's surface, but some very inconspicuous ones are ranged on the lower border. A plant occupies the lower right-hand corner and a bouquet in a very handsome vase, the upper one. Behind Jahangir on a very elaborate chandelier burns a lighted candle, and above his head scales are held by a heavenly being. This is to remind the monarch that he must govern with fairness, and that after judging his subjects, he will see his own actions measured on the scales. This use of a historical subject is another example of tradition inspiring modern carpet weavers.

The lateral borders are occupied by ten portraits of the Great Mughals, six of whom played a particularly important historical role. These are Babur, Humayun, Akbar, Jahangir, Shah Jahan and Aurangzeb. The son of the latter, Bahadur Shah, known also as Shah Alam, came to the throne at the age of sixty-three and was exiled by the British. This sumptuous Mughal period was followed by a half-century of decadence, during which eight emperors reigned, three of whom were assassinated and one deposed. None of these men were great rulers. Among those rulers who continued to reign under the aegis of the British Raj, the most notable were Durah Shah and Razak Shah.

KASHMIR

Date: 1980?
Dimensions: 187 × 134 cm (74 × 53 in)
Asymmetrical knot:
900,000 knots per sq. metre (581 per sq. inch)
   100 knots per 10 cm length (25 per inch length)
    90 knots per 10 cm width (23 per inch width)
Warp of 5 strands of two-ply undyed silk
Weft of 2 strands of undyed silk
Silk pile

The border derives its inspiration from a carpet in the Bostom Museum of Fine Arts, except that here the scrolls bear not human or animal masks, but flowers. It unfolds on a brown ground on which red and blue palmettes alternate, enclosed by large beige, red and green leaves. Two menacing tigers separate and seem to guard the palmettes. The border is channelled between two floral bands; the outer one, with a small red flower between blue ones in quincunx, is particularly attractive.

This rug, recently woven in Kashmir, is an exact replica, somewhat reduced, of an early rug in the collection of the Österreichisches Museum für angewandte Kunst, Vienna. It depicts a rustic scene of the most peaceful and colourful sort, with luxuriant vegetation displayed on a copper-red ground. Along the bottom on a hilly landscape are flowering plants, lilies, begonias and lotus blossoms. Above, a succession of trees spread their branches: some palm-like, others laden with blossom—a captivating scene that inspires feelings of tenderness, and indeed all of the birds inhabiting this sylvan setting are in couples.

In the lower right-hand corner, some parrots are just visible. Higher up, a peacock spreads his tail with obvious vanity before his peahen, while the cockerel, a little beyond, displays his finery. In the centre are two cranes. Turtle-doves and other birds in pairs also savour their good fortune in being together in these idyllic surroundings.

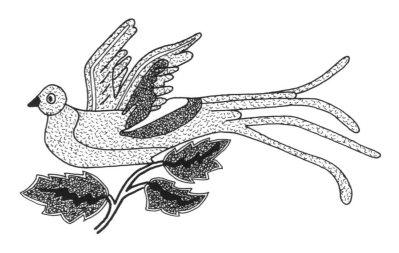

KASHMIR

Date: 1980
Dimensions: 180×123 cm (71×48 in)
Asymmetrical knot:
560,000 knots per sq. metre (361 per sq. inch)
  70 knots per 10 cm length (18 per inch length)
  80 knots per 10 cm width (20 per inch width)
Warp of 4 strands of undyed cotton
Weft of 4 and 2 strands of undyed cotton
Wool and silk pile

This carpet extols the wonders of nature. Its creators—Mohidin and his daughter Farhad—were in tune with the flora and fauna around them and expressed this with the sensitivity of poets.

Indigenous animals frolic on the carpet's rust-coloured field, the tiger chasing the peaceful stag (*uangul*), the muntjak and the wild goat. This pursuit takes place among trees that cover the entire field: flowering almond trees and others, namely the *anar* and the *kikar*. Among these trees the most beautiful birds of Kashmir disport freely: *bulbul*, *myna*, lark, *sapparow*. Flowers and shrubs also take their place on this already well-populated field: jasmine, *panzeen* and *yamberzal*.

The dark blue border bears the same flowers and birds as the field, while running around the narrow inner band are verses expressing popular proverbs: 'the bird that flies high will not be caught by the one that walks, even though he has the same plumage'; 'as long as the soul remains a prisoner of the body, it can find no escape to fly up to heaven'; 'those who love solitude and lead a peaceful life have no reason to fear the attack of an enemy'; 'if you aspire to an honourable life and a good reputation, then you must set your feet on the path of silence and piety'.

KASHMIR

Date: 1982
Dimensions: 210×140 cm (83×55 in)
Asymmetrical knot:
630,000 knots per sq. metre (406 per sq. inch)
 90 knots per 10 cm length (23 per inch length)
 70 knots per 10 cm width (18 per inch width)
Warp of 3 strands of three-ply undyed cotton
Weft of undyed cotton
Wool pile

The province of Kashmir, where the Mughal emperors built their residences, often inspired the artists whom the rulers gathered around them; and so it was that masterpieces glorifying the beauties of this country were produced.

Three centuries have elapsed since the Mughal era. Kashmiri civilization has evolved, but the beauties and natural resources of the country have not changed. Young carpet designers today have at their disposal all the models they require along with the experience bequeathed to them by their elders. With all this behind them, they too produce remarkable carpets.

This example is such a piece. The bouquets ornamenting the medallions and the rosettes occupying the border, interlinked by small buds, have close ties with those of the classical Mughal period.

KASHMIR (detail)

Date: 1982
Dimensions: 276 × 187 cm (109 × 74 in)
Asymmetrical knot:
480,000 knots per sq. metre (310 per sq. inch)
*   80 knots per 10 cm length (20 per inch length)*
*   60 knots per 10 cm width (15 per inch width)*
Warp of 5 strands of undyed cotton
Weft of undyed cotton
Wool pile

This recent product of the Srinagar ateliers could not be more typically Kashmiri. Its colouring betrays its origins, and indeed it is rare to come upon a brown ground in a knotted carpet. Not only the field, but also the border and guard bands are in this colour, and it is certainly true that this palette, with some degree of shading here and there, imparts to the carpet a tranquillity restful to the eye. Early Spanish carpets were similarly coloured, but their knotting was less fine.

The field motifs are simple: crosses with light outlines positioned on flowers cunningly arrayed to emphasize the crosses.

A multitude of rosebuds punctuates the guard bands that enclose the floral border, on which the *boteh-miri* motif is the basic element, its incurved form lending great elegance to the pattern.

AMRITSAR (detail)

Date: 1980
Dimensions: 276×180 cm (109×71 in)
Asymmetrical knot:
480,000 knots per sq. metre (310 per sq. inch)
   80 knots per 10 cm length (20 per inch length)
   60 knots per 10 cm width (15 per inch width)
Warp of 3 strands of three-ply undyed cotton
Weft of blue cotton
Wool pile

Kashmir is the kingdom of flowers and the paradise of birds, each more magnificent than the next. It is no surprise that emigrant Kashmiri artists seeking colourful and graceful models include them so often in their carpet patterns.

Repeated all over the beige field of the carpet is a lozenge with one end slightly swollen, the other gently pinched. It is interesting to note that the surround of the lozenge is not delimited by a gold line forming a lattice within which the motif is commonly inscribed. Here it is simply a white void, a narrow channel, lacking any decorative feature.

Inside the lozenge is an arrangement of ravishing small flowers, to whose stems cling carefree birds, swaying backwards. The border bears a series of small trefoil bouquets, arranged reciprocally, and, together with the six accompanying narrow floral bands, forms a richly profuse frame for this particularly fine carpet.

AMRITSAR

Date: 1980
Dimensions: 200×145 cm (79×57 in)
Asymmetrical knot:
630,000 knots per sq. metre (406 per sq. inch)
*   90 knots per 10 cm length (23 per inch length)*
*   70 knots per 10 cm width (18 per inch width)*
Warp of 3 strands of three-ply undyed cotton
Weft of blue cotton
Wool pile

The arch in this prayer rug recalls a stained-glass window, a vista towards infinity. The wonders of nature spreading out beneath the arch invite the believer at prayer to turn himself towards the Creator.

The free and balanced composition of this rug wins our admiration; it is resplendent with flowers on a red field. The dove standing out at the top of the ogive is not simply a decorative motif, for it serves as the symbol of inner peace administered by divine wisdom to those who open their hearts in prayer. Stunning white and quite plain, the dove contrasts with the sumptuous feathers and colouring of the bird at the base of the field, which probably symbolizes the quest for earthly finery.

The motifs on either side of the apex of the pointed arch focus upon it like two lamps poised to bathe it with light.

The border and five guard bands are beaded with countless tiny flowers in posies or in a sequence of pairs.

AMRITSAR (detail)

Date: 1980
Dimensions: 182×120 cm (72×47 in)
Asymmetrical knot:
200,000 knots per sq. metre (129 per sq. inch)
   50 knots per 10 cm length (13 per inch length)
   40 knots per 10 cm width (10 per inch width)
Warp of 10 strands of undyed cotton
Weft of blue cotton
Wool pile

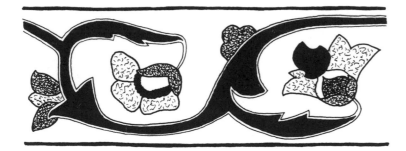

The field of this carpet has a red ground sporting a pretty medallion in the centre. While rather thinly sown on the field, the flowers are perfectly drawn. The attention lavished by the designer on the composition of the spandrel and border becomes apparent in the end of the carpet reproduced opposite.

The dark blue spandrel is separated from the field by an enchanting gold festoon and, strewn with flowers that scintillate like stars on a very dark night, stands out between the red field and light blue ground of the first guard stripe.

A series of beige rosettes circulates around the border, interspersed by small campanula flowers. It is further surrounded by five narrow guard bands with blue, beige or green ground, mostly decorated with attractive floral patterns. Thus the border and guard stripes are a dominant feature of this carpet, though without over-powering the rest of the design.

AMRITSAR (detail)

Date: 1980
Dimensions: 266 × 186 cm (105 × 73 in)
Asymmetrical knot:
300,000 knots per sq. metre (194 per sq. inch)
   60 knots per 10 cm length (15 per inch length)
   50 knots per 10 cm width (13 per inch width)
Warp of 6 strands of undyed cotton
Weft of blue cotton
Wool pile

This is a rug of a rare beauty. The medallion is like a sun that, by diffusing a soft light over the field, highlights all the composite elements, especially the wonderfully drawn flowers.

The white reflections that skirt the pink ground give the medallion the appearance of a jewel of crystalline glass. The medallion serves as a background for a blue star with eight branches—large branches alternating with small ones. Each branch bears an elegant palmette. Lastly, in the centre of the star on a red octagon, as though it were in a casket of velvet, is a green flower—the colour of the queen of gems, the emerald.

To heighten the impact of the central motif there are two small medallions at both its ends, related to the star by their blue ground, red field and decoration of a green flower and finely chased arabesques.

The lightness of the palette and the delicacy of the design of the few flowers that appear on this detail of the field (lilies and lotus blossoms), as well as the palmettes and arabesques, convey an abundance of exceptional richness without becoming oppressive.

AMRITSAR (detail)

Date: 1980
Dimensions: 331×236 cm (130×93 in)
Asymmetrical knot:
300,000 knots per sq. metre (193 per sq. inch)
60 knots per 10 cm length (15 per inch length)
50 knots per 10 cm width (13 per inch width)
Warp of 8 strands of undyed cotton
Weft of blue cotton
Wool pile

This detail once again demonstrates that contrasts, more often than not, are used for emphasis. In general, a light field is highlighted by a dark border; in this piece, however, the opposite occurs. Here, the contrast is violent: an intensely dark blue field framed by a light beige border. But in all carpets the colours of the motifs strengthen or diminish that of the ground, depending on the circumstances and the designer's intentions.

A profusion of flowers fills the entire design. On the field, numerous bouquets sprout from stems that curl and twist around like delicate golden threads. In the border, red, blue and yellow blossoms flutter uninterruptedly, caught in the scrolls of their branches.

Six guard bands (with two types of meanders) add weight to the border, which is too frail to frame this powerful work on its own.

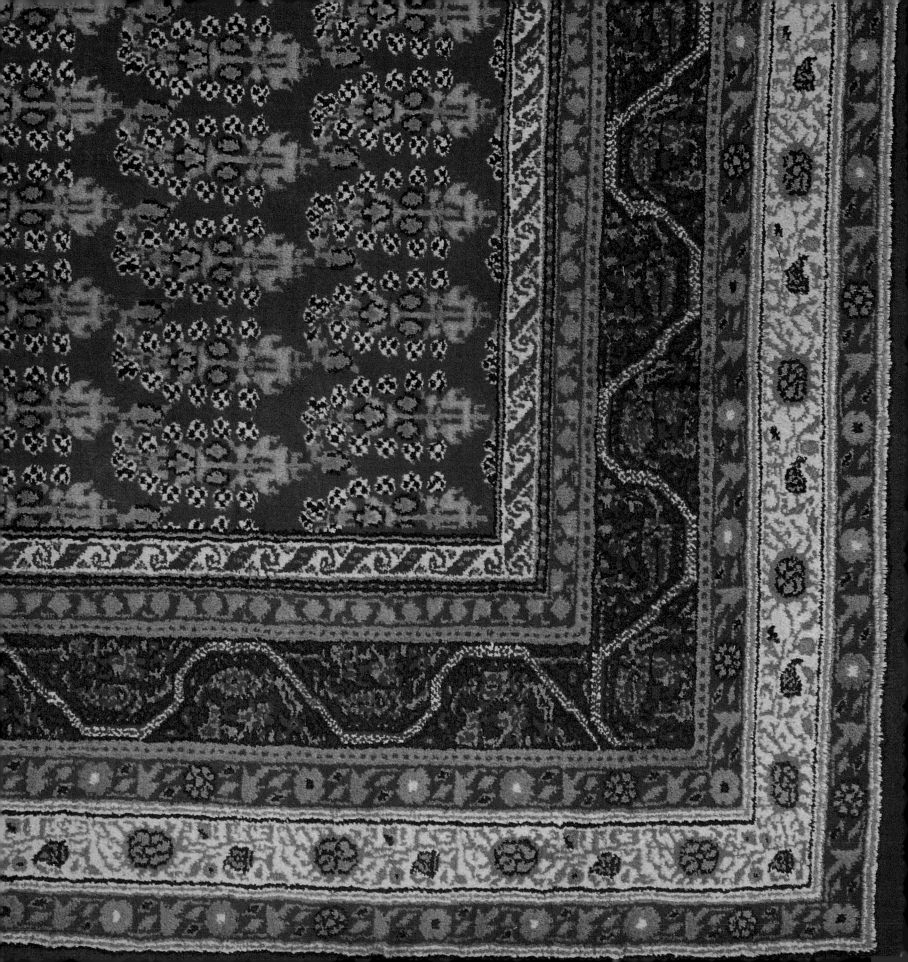

AMRITSAR (detail)

Date: 1980
Dimensions: 249×172 cm (98×68 in)
Asymmetrical knot:
225,000 knots per sq. metre (145 per sq. inch)
*   50 knots per 10 cm length (13 per inch length)*
*   45 knots per 10 cm width (11 per inch width)*
Warp of 7 strands of undyed cotton
Weft of blue cotton
Wool pile

The Kashmiri *boteh-miri*, or princely flower, motif has been used for centuries, having been used to decorate the shawls made there in former days. Other countries adopted the motif to adorn their carpets—Iran in particular, where it was employed in many ways.

The *boteh-miri* appears in this carpet made in Amritsar, where the majority of weavers are Kashmiri. Composed of small elements in blue, green and beige, they fill the red field completely, imparting tranquillity and warmth. Aligned to right and left alternately, these motifs create enough movement to avoid monotony.

Of the many bands that frame the carpet, the wide blue ribbon would seem to be the true border. It is also embellished with *boteh-miri* motifs and flowers with a meander. Another border also stands out in a very light beige with blue flowers scattered at equal distances. The remaining narrow bands are either strewn with flowers or merely plain stripes serving to separate their neighbours.

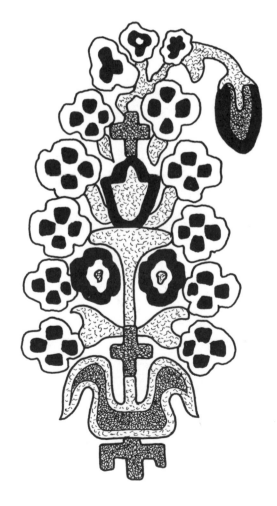

AMRITSAR (detail)

Date: 1980
Dimensions: 300×200 cm (118×79 in)
Asymmetrical knot:
270,000 knots per sq. metre (174 per sq. inch)
*   60 knots per 10 cm length (15 per inch length)*
*   45 knots per 10 cm width (11 per inch width)*
Warp of 8 strands of undyed cotton
Weft of undyed cotton
Wool pile

This rug, with its rust medallion on a cream-coloured ground and rust border framing the ensemble, seems straightforward. It includes, however, some mysterious elements not easy to interpret.

The medallion is a rust-coloured oval bearing in its centre a blue star with eight branches, which are extended by small elongated pendants in cream, each crowned with a red flower.

The motifs ranged above and below the medallion are the subject of controversy: flower petals are clearly present. It is in the nature of ornamentation in the East to embellish traditional forms with fanciful attire in order to arouse both the curiosity and admiration of the spectator.

The rust-coloured border is laden with complex elements composed of palmettes caught within a tracery of scrolls intertwining in all directions; it encroaches on the two blue guard bands alongside, which creates an undulating effect that lightens the carpet's impact.

254

AGRA

Date: 1920
Dimensions: 197 × 124 cm (78 × 49 in)
Asymmetrical knot:
448,000 knots per sq. metre (288 per sq. inch)
    70 knots per 10 cm length (18 per inch length)
    64 knots per 10 cm width (16 per inch width)
Warp of 10 strands of undyed cotton
Weft of 4 strands of blue cotton
Wool pile

This is a wonderful carpet, despite the fact that it is worked in a limited range of colours. The clearly predominant purplish-brown characterizes the production of Agra at a certain period and does not occur in examples from other sources.

Fairly large arabesques, leaves and even *boteh-miri* motifs spread over the field. The skilfully balanced colour scheme of blues, browns and light beige imbues the motifs, and therefore the carpet, with great *élan*. The sky-blue spandrels contain small arabesques.

The beige-brown border, verging on ochre, provides a suitable frame for the field. The border is patterned, in a manner similar to the field, with minutely detailed palmettes, arabesques and *boteh-miri* motifs.

Small flowers are scattered over the two guard stripes that frame the border, one having a pale ground, the other a rust-coloured ground.

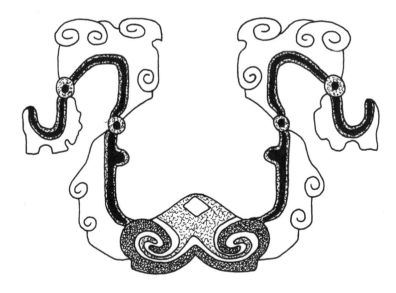

AGRA

Date: 1980
Dimensions: 310×246 cm (122×97 in)
Asymmetrical knot:
240,000 knots per sq. metre (155 per sq. inch)
  60 knots per 10 cm length (15 per inch length)
  40 knots per 10 cm width (10 per inch width)
Warp of 3 strands of two-ply undyed cotton
Weft of 2 strands of two-ply cotton
Wool pile

After a series of carpets inhabited by graceful animals and flowers, this work confronts us with the same elements in a highly stylized form.

Arranged in tiers, three lozenge-shaped medallions, decorated with forms that would seem to be flowers, lie on a red ground that is entirely covered with quasi-geometric motifs, which are none the less suggestive of flowers, palmettes and even domestic animals: peacocks, cockerels and rabbits. In the corner medallions, on a dark blue ground, are other creatures, probably lions with mane and tail.

While the field motifs show the influence of southern Iran, there is none of this in the colouring and framework, which is formed of three borders of equal width separated by narrow bands. Stylized reciprocal motifs that resemble each other pattern the dark blue, red and beige grounds of the bands. Both ends of the carpet bear a supplementary band that lends it an individual character.

AGRA (detail)

Date: 1980
Dimensions: 183 × 119 cm (72 × 47 in)
Asymmetrical knot:
315,000 knots per sq. metre (203 per sq. inch)
* 70 knots per 10 cm length (18 per inch length)*
* 45 knots per 10 cm width (11 per inch width)*
Warp of 6 strands of undyed cotton
Weft of undyed cotton
Wool pile

With reference to the carpet, modern craftsmen, bent on rediscovering the pattern models of the classical period, clothe traditional designs with elements borne of their own genius. Hence, it is easy to recognize the characteristics of the most usual type of modern rugs from Agra. The colour scheme is less vivid than in the past and blends together more attractively and softly. The usual palette consists of rust, beige, cream and white. The knotting is simplified.

This carpet is in the classical mould: large rust-coloured motifs spread over a light field, enclosed by a beige band that follows the shape of the field.

Small flowers enliven the light ground of the rather inconspicuous spandrels. A scrollwork of branches links the rust and beige elements of palmettes and arabesques, which unfurl over the dark border like golden braid on black velvet. The two beige guard bands, dotted with flowers, complete this framework, which has all the appearance of a delicately wrought frieze.

AGRA (detail)

Date: 1980
Dimensions: 272×182 cm (107×72 in)
Asymmetrical knot:
160,000 knots per sq. metre (103 per sq. inch)
* 40 knots per 10 cm length (10 per inch length)*
* 40 knots per 10 cm width (10 per inch width)*
Warp of 4 strands of three-ply undyed cotton
Weft of undyed cotton
Wool pile

Considerable efforts are made nowadays in India to vary carpet patterns. The imagination of the undoubtedly talented designers is clearly in evidence, and like their predecessors—but with new eyes—they know how to observe splendid scenes from nature.

In this detail, the field of the carpet depicts a fine garden or park. Shrubs and trees, cypresses especially, grow from the lower border that is infiltrated by palmettes and flowers, their colours animating the beige ground.

The border stretching between two prettily flowered guard bands contains palmettes, scrolls and flowers, each lying serenely on their own red, blue or blue-black ground. The blue-black ground with scrolls calls to mind a large bird with outspread wings.

AGRA (detail)

Date: 1980
Dimensions: 316 × 244 cm (124 × 96 in)
Asymmetrical knot:
360,000 knots per sq. metre (232 per sq. inch)
*   60 knots per 10 cm length (15 per inch length)*
*   60 knots per 10 cm width (15 per inch width)*
Warp of 5 strands of undyed cotton
Weft of undyed cotton
Wool pile

From the detail reproduced it is possible to reconstruct the whole carpet, for the same motifs are repeated both horizontally and vertically. The designer may simply have allowed his imagination to run riot, reproducing elements of motifs drawn from the treasury of ancestral tradition, transcribed and associated with others at the whim of his imagination—trees, bunches or wreaths of flowers in carefully blended colouring: pink on a blue ground, blue on a yellow ground, or arabesques edged with red or gold.

There is a clear sense of direction in this carpet; all the flower sprays open out towards the top. Furthermore, a harmonious balance is assured by the alignment of the essential motifs in three rows separated by another more modest range of elements.

The border also is an original feature, forming a very airy frame around the well-filled field. Scattered with flowers, the border is patterned with a widely spaced arrangement of alternating foliage and palmettes, separated by leafy garlands that form a basin-like silhouette.

A single green fillet strewn with red flowers edges the outside, while three narrow bands (pink, beige and pink respectively) separate the border from the field like delicate lace.

AGRA

Date: 1980
Dimensions: 192×124 cm (76×49 in)
Asymmetrical knot:
280,000 knots per sq. metre (181 per sq. inch)
  70 knots per 10 cm length (18 per inch length)
  40 knots per 10 cm width (10 per inch width)
Warp of 6 strands of undyed cotton
Weft of undyed cotton
Wool pile

The composition of this prayer rug differs from some other examples (see p. 244), in which the *mihrab* is treated in a manner reminiscent of a stained-glass window depicting floral decorations. Here the *mihrab* faithfully conveys the idea of the columns in a mosque. Unlike other prayer rugs, generally beige and strewn with bright flowers, its dark blue field evokes accurately the penumbra of a mosque in which the faithful seek solitude, the better to enter into the divine mysteries.

All over the field spreads a festoon of petals of incredible variety from the flowers in the vase placed between the columns and from those of the plinth.

The border corresponds in richness to the field and runs between two guard stripes bearing diminutive motifs arranged in a lacy pattern. The beige-brown ground of the border is dotted with equidistant, stylized dark blue flowers.

The gentle palette used on this rug is characteristic of some modern rugs from Agra.

JAIPUR (detail)

Date: 1930
Maharaja Sawai Man Singh II Museum, City Palace, Jaipur
Dimensions: 377×136 cm (148×54 in)
Asymmetrical knot:
360,000 knots per sq. metre (232 per sq. inch)
  60 knots per 10 cm length (15 per inch length)
  60 knots per 10 cm width (15 per inch width)
Warp of 6 strands of undyed cotton
Weft of beige cotton
Wool pile

The border unfolds between two ochre-coloured guard stripes on which is a spirited arrangement of pretty red and blue flowers, interlinked by smaller ones.

Who would imagine that this carpet was woven in the prison at Jaipur? The story behind this began in 1856, when Maharaja Sawai Ram Singh II (1835-80) decided to procure a trade for the prisoners to prevent them sinking into idleness and to help them to earn a living after serving their sentence. He repaired the old prison, built a new one and established a weaving workshop, improving the conditions of detention in the process. Workshops were functioning by 1864, producing not only knotted carpets but also kilim weaves, embroidered felts and materials for clothing or furnishings. These rugs very rapidly acquired a high reputation and were greatly sought after. The example shown here is finely knotted and of pleasing design.

On the field of the carpet, a number of birds savour their good fortune at living in such a beautiful garden. The prisoners must have enjoyed the illusion of freedom while weaving this varicoloured array of flowers and palmettes in light beige, pink and dark blue.

269

JAIPUR

Date: 1980
Dimensions: 185×121 cm (73×48 in)
Asymmetrical knot:
337,500 knots per sq. metre (218 per sq. inch)
*   75 knots per 10 cm length (19 per inch length)*
*   45 knots per 10 cm width (11 per inch width)*
Warp of 6 strands of undyed cotton
Weft of undyed cotton
Wool pile

This carpet from the Jaipur workshops illustrates the policy adopted by the present-day designers of this town, who choose traditional motifs, somewhat modified in line and sequence, and opt for a very soft palette in which brown and beige predominate.

As the field subtly suggests, this is a prayer rug. The *mihrab* is only vaguely indicated by the light grass at the base of the field and the equally light upper corners of ogival form, behind dark scrolls.

A wide spray of flowers grows from a skilfully fashioned vase set on a plinth on the lower border. These blooms spread over the centre of the field and, given added impact by scattered dark flowers, serve as a sort of medallion. The bouquet divides towards the top to fall in pale green clusters that then splay out all over the field—an unusual touch.

The dark blue border constitutes an original frame in which wonderfully drawn interlinking scrolls enclose flowers and palmettes; such precision demands very fine knotting. Two pairs of narrow bands contain the border, the inner pair being in the form of a meander composed of a series of small motifs.

JAIPUR

Date: 1980
Dimensions: 190×125 cm (75×49 in)
Asymmetrical knot:
320,000 knots per sq. metre (206 per sq. inch)
   80 knots per 10 cm length (20 per inch length)
   40 knots per 10 cm width (10 per inch width)
Warp of 6 strands of undyed cotton
Weft of undyed cotton
Wool pile

The artist who conceived this design—an unenclosed aviary—probably drew his inspiration from the province of Rajasthan where there is a bird sanctuary unique in the world.

On the light ground of the rug, scored by flowering branches, countless birds pose prettily, displaying the colours of their plumage. Those occupying the medallion are shown to best advantage against the strong red ground.

The border is in the same tone as the central motif and punctuated by elongated medallions, separated like spots of light by pretty golden rosettes. Two light guard bands frame the red border. An additional narrow stripe with wavy floral pattern separates the field from the inner guard in order to distinguish the two areas with similar light backgrounds.

JAIPUR

Date: 1980
Dimensions: 195×123 cm (77×48 in)
Asymmetrical knot:
280,000 knots per sq. metre (181 per sq. inch)
  70 knots per 10 cm length (18 per inch length)
  40 knots per 10 cm width (10 per inch width)
Warp of 7 strands of undyed cotton
Weft of undyed cotton
Wool pile

The impression given by this carpet is one of perfect
unity: unity both of design, in which all lines converge on
the centre, and of tone, in which colours contrast or blend
very subtly.

The centre of the carpet is formed of three lacy
medallions, overlaid one upon the other and distinguished from each other only in colouring. This triple
motif that guides the eye of the beholder to the centre of
the carpet is reinforced by the dark blue field, in the form
of a medallion strewn with flowers, on which it rests.

Bunches of flowers intertwine in the corners of the
field, while along the border small blue rosettes alternate
with larger beige ones.

274

JAIPUR (detail)

Date: 1980
Dimensions: 190×122 cm (75×48 in)
Asymmetrical knot:
240,000 knots per sq. metre (155 per sq. inch)
* 60 knots per 10 cm length (15 per inch length)*
* 40 knots per 10 cm width (10 per inch width)*
Warp of 6 strands of undyed cotton
Weft of undyed cotton
Wool pile

This is another example of a carpet with the field entirely covered with the same motif. A stylized flower trapped behind a golden grille is repeated in perfect alignment both vertically and horizontally. The designer wished to create a calm and tranquil surface. With no highly elaborate motifs or over-subtle arrangements, the beauty of this carpet is derived from its moderation. Thus, it allows any piece of furniture placed on or near it to be seen to its best effect.

The border, a copper-red path with a pattern of alternating flowers and scrolls, forcefully encloses this intentionally delicate field.

BHADOHI (detail)

Date: 1980
Dimensions: 298×241 cm (117×95 in)
Asymmetrical knot:
200,000 knots per sq. metre (129 per sq. inch)
   50 knots per 10 cm length (13 per inch length)
   40 knots per 10 cm width (10 per inch width)
Warp of 4 strands of three-ply undyed cotton
Weft of 2 strands of blue cotton
Wool pile

In their efforts to intensify the effect of a carpet's field, designers may diminish the importance of the frame, that is to say the strength of the colouring and the width of the border and guard bands, or reinforce them. The author of this design chose the second option.

The wonderful light beige field is resplendent with flowers and foliage growing on such slender stems that seem to dance attendance on the medallion set in the centre. The latter is minutely spiked all around its circumference and balanced by two floral shapes laterally and longitudinally. Dark in colour, its centre marked with two rotated crosses, the medallion contains an arrangement of small multicoloured flowers of rare beauty.

Around the field are a succession of ever darker borders. The first border of pale green is in a floral style similar to the field and only slightly darker. It is a step towards the next border, the true frame, which is full of varied motifs of great stateliness and stretches between two triple bands. This is in itself an enchanting design that plainly manifests the exceptional talent of the designer. Palmettes, each encircled by two stems that seem to bear rosebuds and protected by two leaping antelopes, follow one another at some distance, engagingly linked by small clusters of delightful flowers.

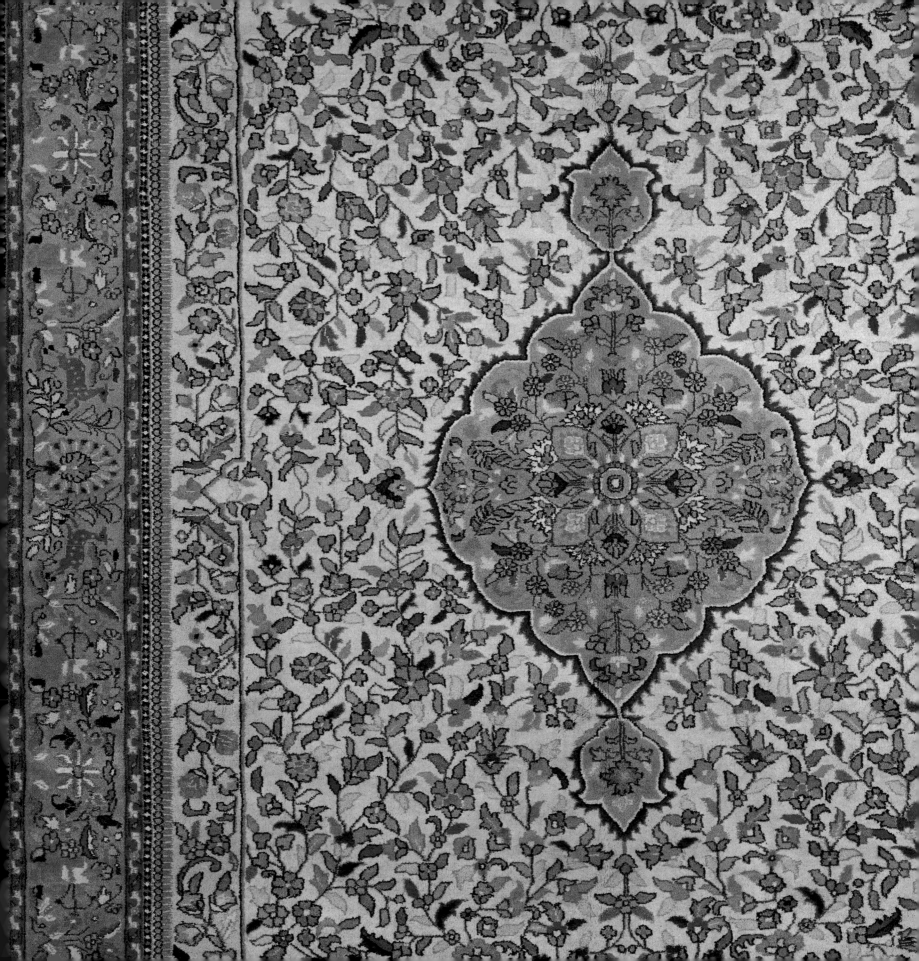

BHADOHI (detail)

Date: 1980
Dimensions: 334 × 244 cm (131 × 96 in)
Asymmetrical knot:
330,000 knots per sq. metre (213 per sq. inch)
*   60 knots per 10 cm length (15 per inch length)*
*   55 knots per 10 cm width (14 per inch width)*
Warp of 3 strands of three-ply undyed cotton
Weft of undyed cotton
Wool pile

The reproduction of a small area reveals wonderful minutiae that could not be observed if the whole carpet were shown greatly reduced. The scrolls of branches smothered with flowers and foliage are admirable on the light field. Random palmettes and floral motifs form focal points and link the whole composition together.

The border and field have the same ground-colour, but are isolated from each other by four adjacent bands that bear small devices of flowers and single lines on a red or blue ground. On the border proper is a series of scrolls and palmettes running between clearly emphasized volutes.

BHADOHI (detail)

Date: 1980
Dimensions: 349×258 cm (137×102 in)
Asymmetrical knot:
220,000 knots per sq. metre (142 per sq. inch)
*   55 knots per 10 cm length (14 per inch length)*
*   40 knots per 10 cm width (10 per inch width)*
Warp of 3 strands of four-ply undyed cotton
Weft of undyed cotton
Wool pile

Even this small detail allows us a glimpse of the beauty of this piece, its clarity, delicacy and—most strikingly—the attention to detail.

The beige field is charmingly and subtly covered with a wide range of flowers of all colours, sprawling in all directions on narrow stems.

The twin borders—one on a red ground, the other on blue—enclose the field in an impressive frame, with a succession of palmettes and arabesques among a skilfully organized network of flowers and tendrils. The borders run between three triple guard bands, the central one beaded with dainty flower buds.

The eight-pointed star in each of the four corners of the wide outer border is also a notable feature.

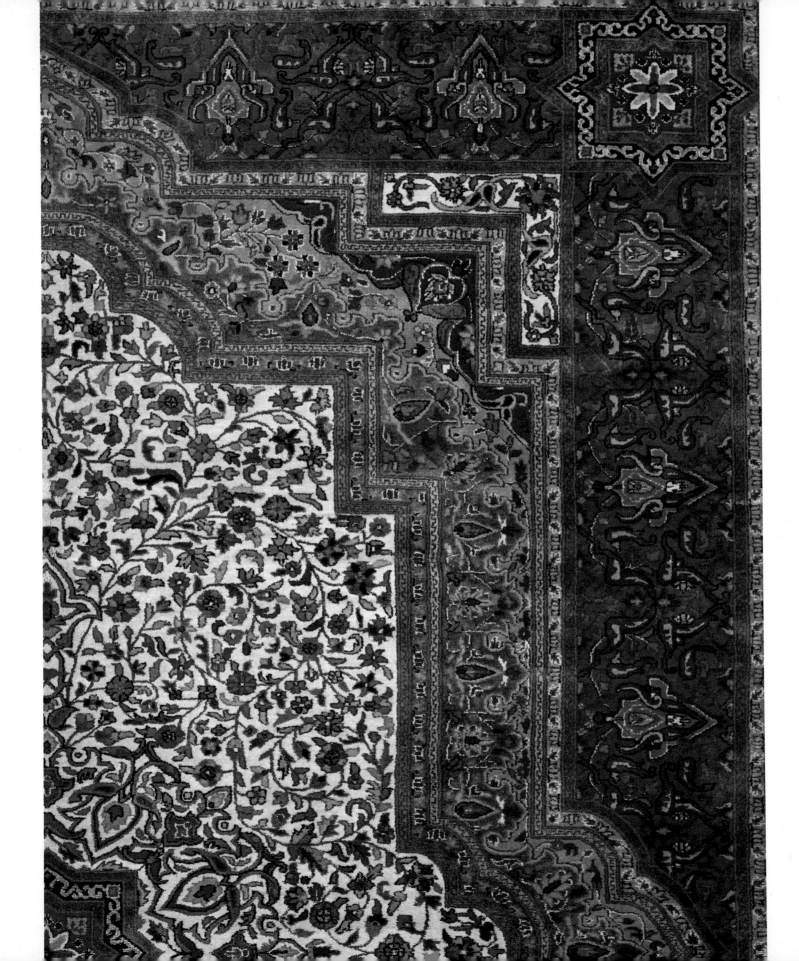

BHADOHI

Date: 1980
Dimensions: 308×240 cm (121×94 in)
Asymmetrical knot:
157,500 knots per sq. metre (102 per sq. inch)
  45 knots per 10 cm length (11 per inch length)
  35 knots per 10 cm width (9 per inch width)
Warp of 3 strands of four-ply undyed cotton
Weft of undyed cotton
Wool pile

Examples of carpets having a sky-blue ground for the field are uncommon. The cream-coloured medallion, containing an octagonal ornament—like a jewel in a finely chased mount—is set proudly to advantage in the centre.

The field is strewn with a myriad of small multi-coloured flowers. Around the field, like a picture frame, runs a beige-brown band with tiny flowers.

The border proper is very lively. Among flowers and shrubs punctuated by charming palmettes, hunters lying in wait aim their bows at unwary does. This exuberant border is edged on each side with three narrow stripes.

BHADOHI (detail)

Date: 1980
Dimensions: 349×251 cm (137×99 in)
Asymmetrical knot:
360,000 knots per sq. metre (232 per sq. inch)
  60 knots per 10 cm length (15 per inch length)
  60 knots per 10 cm width (15 per inch width)
Warp of 3 strands of two-ply undyed cotton
Weft of 3 strands of two-ply undyed cotton
Wool pile

This carpet is a veritable flower-bed. Although a certain order can be found in the arrangement of the posies and bunches of flowers, the absence of well-defined motifs and cross-patterning creates an illusion of freedom. Infinitely varied flowers appear to grow wherever they fancy. This diversity of shapes and colours fills the field with so much life that the absence of motifs with well-defined contours does not seem important.

The border, of more elaborate appearance, with flowers and scrolls sprouting from leafy stems, is framed by two pairs of floral bands of the same blue as is found in the foliage of the border and the field.

BHADOHI (detail)

Date: 1980
Dimensions: 293×204 cm (115×80 in)
Asymmetrical knot:
105,000 knots per sq. metre (68 per sq. inch)
   35 knots per 10 cm length (9 per inch length)
   30 knots per 10 cm width (8 per inch width)
Warp of 6 strands of undyed cotton
Weft of grey cotton
Wool pile

Despite the apparent presence of an occasional rosette forming a part of a motif, this carpet is of linear composition. The motifs are repeated and interlocked, forming a mosaic that could serve as the decorative element for either a wall or a floor. The quiet background of this rug could provide a setting for a work of art without any hint of discord—and, indeed, this is another role of carpets.

The border, marked out with a succession of square motifs bearing varied patterns, is reminiscent of a ceramic frieze. It winds between quadruple guard bands that facilitate the passage from the border, with its striking elements, to the serene field of the carpet.

BHADOHI

Date: 1980
Dimensions: 353×252 cm (139×99 in)
Asymmetrical knot:
330,000 knots per sq. metre (213 per sq. inch)
*   60 knots per 10 cm length (15 per inch length)*
*   55 knots per 10 cm width (14 per inch width)*
Warp of 3 strands of three-ply undyed cotton
Weft of undyed cotton
Wool pile

With no central medallion or lattice to orientate the design, nor any dominant motifs, there are hardly any landmarks to serve as an aid in deciphering the symmetry that governs the arrangement of this myriad of elements—a world of flowers presented for inspection in a sober yet rich pattern.

The warmth of the red field recalls the carpets of the Mughal period. Beige plays a predominant role, entering into the structure of all motifs, however tiny, either as the essential component, where it creates a splash of light, or as a background colour, that permits other tones to express themselves strongly by contrast.

The flowers are either in bunches, in clusters or blossoming on tenuous leafy stems. Although they are accurately drawn, it would be pointless to attempt to identify them all.

The border is more visibly coordinated and provides an appropriately solid frame for the field. It is a peaceful blue band bearing equidistant palmettes and lilies, the foliage of the latter serving as a link between the palmettes. Chains of flower buds pattern the gold and pale blue ground of the two guard stripes.

BHADOHI

Date: 1980
Dimensions: 303×241 cm (119×95 in)
Asymmetrical knot:
160,000 knots per sq. metre (103 per sq. inch)
   40 knots per 10 cm length (10 per inch length)
   40 knots per 10 cm width (10 per inch width)
Warp of 3 strands of four-ply undyed cotton
Weft of blue cotton
Wool pile

This is an original piece on all counts, from the motifs to the brownish-beige colouring. It calls to mind a huge slab of marble paving, set into a plain-coloured floor.

Three medallions, embedded into each other, occupy the middle of the field and project beyond it. Right at the centre the smallest device—a reduced version of the other two—is the gem of this carpet. The second medallion, along with the frame of the border (which is also dark in colour), forms the carpet's skeleton and, consequently, is responsible for its equilibrium. The points of the third medallion, a deep-beige lozenge, are thrust into the border. The floral branches of the border reciprocate this encroachment by invading the field in their turn.

Flowers are in evidence everywhere, in red, pink, blue and white, scattered in profusion as in a flower-bed or sprouting from delicate stems that undulate like gold wire.

Large palmettes occupy the corners of the border, which unfolds between seven narrow bands.

BHADOHI

Date: 1980
Dimensions: 159×89 cm (63×35 in)
Asymmetrical knot:
350,000 knots per sq. metre (226 per sq. inch)
   50 knots per 10 cm length (13 per inch length)
   70 knots per 10 cm width (18 per inch width)
Warp of 3 strands of two-ply undyed cotton
Weft of 4 strands of undyed cotton
Wool pile

This prayer rug has the appearance of a sunlit window through which one contemplates the floral arrangement in a flower vase.

A bouquet of varied flowers, in which tulips apparently predominate, is contained in an extremely slender and finely decorated vase occupying the centre of the field. From small grassy hills at both sides of the lower border rise two branches that skirt the sides of the field, ornamenting them with flowers and foliage, before they meet at the summit.

Reciprocal blue palmettes, interlinked by small, triple-flowered posies, are arranged on a copper-red ground in the spandrels and principal border. Three blue and gold bands form the guard stripes.

BHADOHI

Date: 1980
Dimensions: 192×136 cm (76×54 in)
Asymmetrical knot:
300,000 knots per sq. metre (194 per sq. inch)
  50 knots per 10 cm length (13 per inch length)
  60 knots per 10 cm width (15 per inch width)
Warp of 2 strands of three-ply undyed cotton
Weft of 4 strands of undyed cotton
Wool pile

The beige field of this prayer rug was conceived with the intention of filling with joy and light the believer who knelt upon it to pray—with light through the scintillating clarity of the beige ground, and with joy through the lavish profusion of the flowers.

Although the central spray rises from an unobtrusive vase and the flowers are arranged with some order, the fact that the stems are not visible creates the illusion of a free design. Flowers of a multitude of species, packed together closely, are depicted in their habitual colouring. Their numbers bear witness to the prodigious abundance of creation.

Similar flowers appear in the upper sections of the copper-red field, with floral medallions in the corners. The dark blue border is patterned by palmettes shrouded by carnations, lilies, lotus blossoms and small clusters of seven pink or white blooms. It unfolds between two golden bands, dotted with enchanting flower buds.

MIRZAPUR

Date: 1980
Dimensions: 230×194 cm (91×76 in)
Asymmetrical knot:
160,000 knots per sq. metre (103 per sq. inch)
40 knots per 10 cm length (10 per inch length)
40 knots per 10 cm width (10 per inch width)
Warp of 3 strands of four-ply undyed cotton
Weft of 8 strands of undyed cotton
Wool pile

The lattice that encloses the medallions on this carpet was already encountered previously on the early Mughal rugs, but in more elaborate form. The motifs inside the medallions are also quite different from Mughal carpets. In early pieces the bouquets are all varied, while these contain well-ordered beds of completely identical flowers around small central motifs in beige or brown. The colour of the field is also novel. Whereas previously it had been of Mughal red, here it is brick red.

Finally, the border which is bounded by two double floral guards (the inner ones dark, the other ones light) is also an innovation. Somewhat unobtrusive palmettes on a carpet of flowers are separated by elongated and heavily outlined pairs of leaves, like the wings of birds, which form a striking chain within the border.

MIRZAPUR

Date: 1980
Dimensions: 289 × 190 cm (114 × 75 in)
Asymmetrical knot:
200,000 knots per sq. metre (129 per sq. inch)
 50 knots per 10 cm length (13 per inch length)
 40 knots per 10 cm width (10 per inch width)
Warp of 12 strands of undyed cotton
Weft of blue cotton
Wool pile

This is a carpet that must be examined very closely to discover its hidden beauty. The large motifs such as the dark blue central lozenge or the S-shaped leaves all over the surface should not be allowed to monopolize our attention, for they conceal so many wonders.

The large dark lozenge is divided into small versions of itself, each with a decorated surround. Each contains a small ochre medallion enclosing three flowers; the same medallion also appears in the central beige lozenge and in those in the corners of the field. Apart from this motif, the entire field is nothing more than a vast flower-bed of small yellow, pink, beige and blue blooms. Although small in scale, they are graceful and finely worked.

The border is formed of a succession of sprigs of tiny flowers in fan-tail formation, shaded by large fronds that open out in pairs like the wings of a bird. The border is enclosed by double guard stripes, the intermediary pair beaded with flowers in the traditional manner. But the other two are more imaginative, especially the festooned inner band, which encroaches attractively onto the field, adding to the charm of the frame.

GLOSSARY

ABRASH
Word used in the carpet trade to denote streaks in the shading of the main colour of a carpet. These streaks, of varying intensities of colour, result from the method of drying dyed wool in the sun. The wool is dried in piles, and the wool at the bottom dries in darker shades than that at the top, not only because it is not exposed to the fading influence of the sun's rays but also because some dye seeps down through the pile of wool.

ARABESQUE
Stylized curving ornament that is derived from the acanthus leaf. The term applies to all complex linear decoration based on curved lines.

BORDER
The frame of a carpet and an immutable convention of carpet design. It usually consists of a wider middle element—the actual border—with one, two or more narrow guard bands or stripes.

BOTEH-MIRI MOTIF
This is one of several versions of the *boteh* or serrated-leaf design which originated in India and was adopted throughout the Orient. The words *boteh-miri* come from the Farsi for 'princely flower'. Experts differ on what the motif represents: a pine, a palm, a cluster of leaves or the sacred flame of Zoroaster.

CARTOON
Village weavers were unable to weave the intricate floral and animal designs for large carpets drawn by court painters. A new technique was therefore evolved, the use of which greatly facilitated the weaving of carpets with very elaborate designs: a designer prepares on paper a preliminary large-scale sketch of the design to be woven; squares (each representing a knot) are then ruled on the sketch by hand, some workers being employed solely for this purpose. The sketch on squared paper is the cartoon, and the method is still in use today.

CLOUDBAND MOTIF
A small, shell-like motif occurring in various forms, some compressed, some elongated. It is thought to represent a single cloud but, in fact, resembles the conventional Chinese 'bank of clouds' motif. The motif is the symbol of immortality and of the elixir of long life, also called the *lingzhi* ('sacred fungus' or 'sacred sponge') or the *chi* motif.

EIGHT-POINTED STAR MOTIF
A motif found on carpets woven by Muslims, who borrowed the design—a symbol of divinity—and named it 'jewel of Muhammad'. According to legend, King Solomon wore an eight-pointed diamond, the 'Star of the Medes' on his finger, and that is another term for this motif.

FIELD
Term for the part of the carpet within the borders.

FLOWER-BED
A rectangular decoration placed above and below the *mihrab* of prayer rugs.

FRINGE

Decorative border or edging on a carpet, composed of the visible, hanging ends of the warp threads that have been trimmed and knotted.

GROUND (or BACKGROUND)

The general surface of a rug on which the designs are arranged to provide relief for the principal motifs.

GUARD BAND or STRIPE

The narrow band or bands flanking the wider border in the framing of a carpet.

KNOT: ASYMMETRICAL

A type of pile knot tied on two adjacent warp threads; only one of the warp threads is encircled by the strand of wool, the other merely being interlaced so that the two ends of the strand reappear separately: the first between one of the two warp threads mentioned, and the second between one of these and the following warp thread. This knot, also called the Persian or Senneh knot, can be tied equally well from right to left or vice versa and is thus sometimes termed the 'two-handed knot'. (See p. 26).

LOTUS MOTIF

The nelumbo or Indian lotus, as an open flower or bud, used as a motif in carpets. The lotus is a sacred flower for Buddhists and represents purity, creative power and fertility, as well as being the symbol for summer.

LOZENGE MOTIF

A motif in the shape of a diamond.

MEDALLION

A motif, often round or oval, confined to the centre of the field of a rug. Many carpets have a design consisting of a large central medallion, a quarter of which reappears in each corner of the field.

MIHRAB

Design characteristic of prayer rugs and derived from the chamber or prayer niche in a mosque that indicates the direction of Mecca. The upper part of the *mihrab* has sides which slope up to the summit that culminates in a point or arch that must point towards Mecca while the worshipper prays on his rug.

MOSQUE-LAMP MOTIF

A realistic or stylized lamp hanging on a chain suspended from the point of the *mihrab*'s arch. Often found on prayer rugs, this motif is reminiscent of similar lamps that hang in mosques.

PALMETTE MOTIF

A motif in the shape of a honeysuckle, probably derived from the flower of the Egyptian or Chinese lotus.

PILE

The mass of raised tufts formed by cutting the strands of wool knotted around the warp threads. The pile provides the soft, compact, furry surface of the carpet.

POMEGRANATE MOTIF

For the tribes of eastern Turkestan this fruit symbolizes fertility. In other parts of China and for Buddhists, the pomegranate is a symbol of a propitious influence. Both the fruit and the tree are used as motifs to decorate oriental rugs.

PRAYER RUG
Small oriental rug used by Muslims to kneel on when saying their daily prayers. Prayer rugs are characteristically decorated with a *mihrab*.

ROSETTE MOTIF
A motif resembling an open rose with the petals arranged in a circle around the centre.

'S' MOTIF
Motif of very early origin in the shape of an 'S'; generally assumed to be connected with sun worship and symbolizing light, divinity and wisdom.

SELVEDGE
The edge on either side of a woven fabric, so finished as to prevent the ravelling of the weft. The selvedge is often woven of different or heavier threads than the fabric and sometimes in a different weave.

SPANDREL
The ornamentally treated corner of a rug between a round field and a rectangular border. Spandrels are filled with figures, scrolls or other motifs, and elements of the central medallion are often repeated in its decoration.

TALIM
A roll of paper marked with a code (see pp. 20, 25) indicating the number of knots to be woven in their respective colours. This is a typical Kashmiri manner of transmitting the pattern to the weavers.

TREE-OF-LIFE MOTIF
This motif of a tree (which may be highly stylized) is often found on prayer rugs because of its religious significance for Islam. It is one of mankind's oldest symbols of life.

WARP
The yarn stretched vertically on a hand-knotted carpet. The knots forming the pile are tied on the warp threads.

WEFT
The yarn that the weaver passes across the width of the carpet between the warp threads. The weft threads maintain the knots of the pile in place.

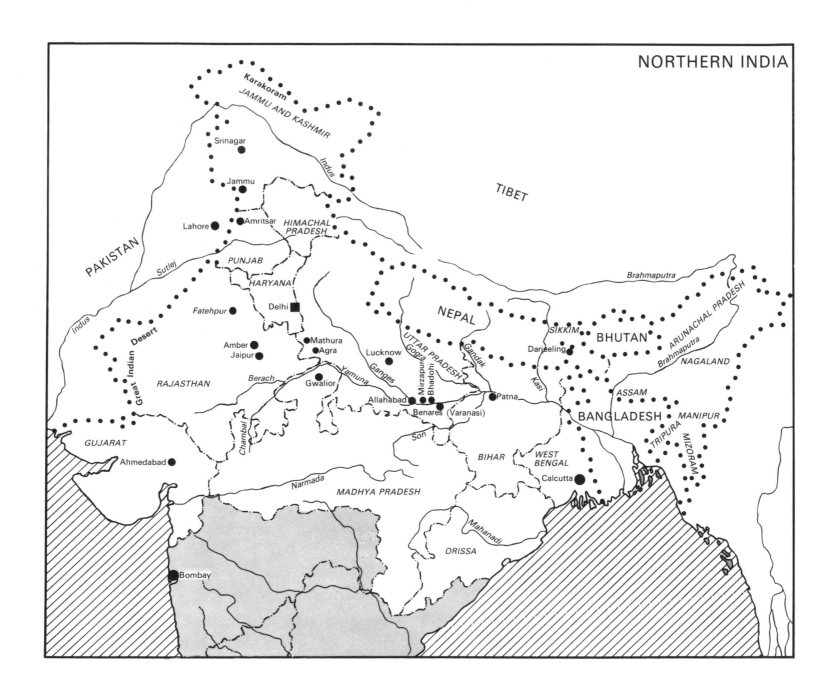

NORTHERN INDIA

BIBLIOGRAPHY

Banerjei, N.N. *Monograph on the Woollen Fabrics of Bengal*. Calcutta, 1899.

Beattie, May H. *The Thyssen-Bornemisza Collection of Oriental Rugs*. Castagnola, 1972.

Black, A. and C. *Oriental Carpets, Runners and Rugs and Some Jacquard Reproductions*. London, 1900.

Brendon, B.A. *A Monograph on the Woollen Fabrics of the Bombay Presidency*. Bombay, 1899.

Campana, P. Michele. *Il Tappeto Orientale*. Milan, 1945.

— *Oriental Carpets*. Trans. by A. Hartcup. London and New York, 1969.

Chattopadhyaya, Kamaladevi. *Carpets and Floor Coverings of India*. Bombay, 1969.

Dilley, Arthur U. *Oriental Carpets and Rugs: A Comprehensive Study*. Philadelphia and New York, 1931; Rev. ed. by M.S. Dimand. New York, 1959.

Dimand, Maurice S. and Mailey, Jean. *Oriental Rugs in the Metropolitan Museum of Art*. New York, 1973.

Dowson, John. *Classical Dictionary of Hindu Mythology and Religion*. London, 1961; reprinted London, 1972.

Enthoven, R.E. *The Cotton Fabrics of the Bombay Presidency*. Bombay, 1897.

Erdmann, Kurt. *Der indische Knüpfteppich*. Göttingen, 1959.

— *Siebenhundert Jahre Orientteppich: Zu seiner Geschichte und Erforschung*. Foreword by Hanna Erdmann. Herford, 1966.

Gans-Ruedin, Erwin. *Modern Oriental Carpets*. Trans. by Valerie Howard. London and Rutland, VT, 1971.

— *Antique Oriental Carpets*. Trans. by Elizabeth and Richard Bartlett. New York and London, 1975.

— *The Great Book of Oriental Carpets*. Trans. by Valerie Howard. New York, 1983.

Griggs, William. *Illustrations of the Textile Manufacturers of India*. London, 1881.

Guide to the Collection of Carpets. London: Victoria and Albert Museum, 1915; 1920; 1931.

Harris, Henry T. *Monograph on the Carpet Weaving Industry of Southern India*. Madras, 1908.

Hendley, Thomas H. *Asian Carpets: 16th and 17th Century*. London, 1905.

Hennessy, John Gerard. *Central Carpets of Peshawar*. Lahore, 1916.

Irwin, John. 'Early Indian Carpets'. In *Antiques* LXIX (New York, 1956): 154-7.

— *The Girdlers' Carpet*. London, 1962.

— *The Paisley Shawl*. London, 1973.

Iten-Maritz, J. *Enzyklopädie des Orientteppichs*. Herford, 1977.

Johnstone, D.C. *Monograph on Woollen Manufacturers of the Punjab*. Lahore, 1884-5.

Kendrick, A.F. and Tattersall, C.E.C. *Fine Carpets in the Victoria and Albert Museum*. London, 1924.

Latimer, C. *Monograph on Carpet Making in the Punjab.* Lahore, 1905-6.

McMullan, Joseph V. *Islamic Carpets.* New York, 1965.

Martin, F.R. *A History of Oriental Carpets before 1800.* Vienna, 1906-8.

Mehta, J.R. *The Handicrafts and Industrial Arts of India.* Bombay, 1960.

Mehta, P.N. *Report of the Handloom Industry.* Bombay, 1909.

Mukerji, N.G. *A Monograph of Carpet Weaving in Bengal.* Calcutta, 1907.

Neugebauer, R. and Orendi, J. *Handbuch der orientalischen Teppichkunde.* Leipzig, 1909.

Orendi, J. *Das Gesamtwissen über antike und neue Teppiche des Orients.* Vienna, 1930.

Pima, A.W. *A Monograph on Woollen Fabrics in the North-Western Provinces and Oudh.* Allahabad, 1898.

Sarre, F. and Trenkwald, H. *Altorientalische Teppiche.* 2 vols. Vienna and Leipzig, 1926-8.
— *Old Oriental Carpets.* Trans. by A.F. Kendrick. Vienna and Leipzig, 1926-9.

Schlosser, Ignaz. *Tapis d'Orient et d'Occident.* Fribourg, 1962.

Silberrod, C.A. *A Monograph on Cotton Fabrics Produced in the North-Western Provinces and Oudh.* Allahabad, 1898.

Skelton, Robert. *The Indian Heritage: Court Life and Arts under Mughal Rule.* London, 1982.

Smith, Vincent A. *The Early History of India.* Oxford, 1908.

Spear, Percival and Thapar, Romila. *A History of India.* 2 vols. London, 1965-6.

Spühler, Friedrich. *Islamic Carpets and Textiles in the Keir Collection.* London, 1978.

Teppich Erzeugung im Orient. Vienna: K.K. Österreichisches Handelsmuseum, 1895.

Thurston, Edgar. *Monograph on the Woollen Fabric Industry of the Madras Presidency.* Madras, 1898.

Twigg, H.J.R. *A Monograph on the Art and Practice of Carpet Making in the Bombay Presidency.* Bombay, 1907.

Watson, Francis. *A Concise History of India.* London, 1974.

Watt, Sir G. *Commercial Products of India.* London, 1908.
— *Indian Art at Delhi.* Calcutta, 1903.

Zipper, K. *Orientteppiche, das Lexikon.* Brunswick, 1970.

ACKNOWLEDGMENTS

The author wishes to thank for their valuable help:
Mr. Narendra Singh, the Indian Ambassador in Paris;
Mr. Gyan Prakash, New Delhi;
Mr. J.M. Mengi, Srinagar;
Shri Gulam Russull Khan, Srinagar;
Mr. A.M. and Mr. M.M. Bisati, Srinagar;
Dr. A.K. Das, Jaipur;
Mr. B.S. Paul, New Delhi;
Mr. Harpal Singh, Amritsar;
Mr. Nashu Chelleram, Bombay;
Mr. H.K. Wattal, Agra.
Gérard Aubry took charge of all administration.

PHOTO CREDITS

The publishers wish to thank all the photographers who collaborated on this book, as well as the museums and other institutions which supplied additional photographic material. The illustrations not listed below were photographed by Leo Hilber, Fribourg. The photo research for this book was done by Ingrid de Kalbermatten.

Patrick Berger, Tavannes   Pls. 11, 28 29
India Tourist Office, Geneva   Pls. 2, 3, 8, 9, 10, 13, 26, 27
Keir Collection   pp. 108, 112, 120, 144
   (photos: P.J. Gates Ltd, London)
Xavier Lecoultre   Pls. 12, 20, 21, 30

Boston, Museum of Fine Arts   p. 68
Castagnola, Thyssen-Bornemisza Collection   pp. 115, 116, 119
Detroit, Institute of Arts   p. 128
Düsseldorf, Kunstmuseum   p. 135
   (photo: Landesbildstelle Rheinland, Düsseldorf)
Glasgow, Glasgow Museums and Art Galleries, Burrell Collection   p. 71
Hamburg, Museum für Kunst und Gewerbe   p. 140
   (photo: Marion Höflinger, Hamburg)
Istanbul, Türk ve Islam Eserleri Müzesi   p. 111
   (photo: Reha Günay, Istanbul)
London, The Girdlers' Company   p. 72
   (photo: Eileen Tweedy, London)
London, Victoria and Albert Museum   pp. 75, 136
Lyons, Musée historique des Tissus   p. 84
New York, Frick Collection   p. 123
New York, Metropolitan Museum of Art   pp. 79, 83, 124, 127, 143
Vienna, Österreichisches Museum für angewandte Kunst   pp. 76, 80
Washington, D.C., National Gallery of Art   pp. 63, 64
Washington, D.C., Textile Museum   pp. 67, 139

Author's archives   Pls. 1, 4, 5, 7

INDEX

This book was printed and bound in August, 1984 by
Buchdruckerei und Verlag Busse, Herford.
Photolithography: Buchdruckerei und Verlag Busse, Herford.
Setting: Transfotexte, Lausanne.

Printed and bound in West Germany